CONTENTS

CONTENTS

My grandfather was a German immigrant, complete with his big, plush German Shepherd, King. When we had our regular visit to Grandad's place, I would be found outside playing with this magnificent animal, tugging on his neck and hugging him as though he were a stuffed toy. We were friends.

My fascination for the breed never wavered, and when I got my first after-school job, I started saving, not for a car, but for a dog. Finally, at 15 years of age I had saved enough and the family jumped into our old Chevy and was off to the Rin Tin Tin Kennels in Riverside, CA.

Heidi was not a show dog, but she was the fulfillment of the dreams of a young boy watching *The Adventures of Rin Tin Tin* on TV while rehearsing in my mind the adventures that would someday come to me. And they did. Heidi and I were off in search of a world to conquer and unknown territories to explore. She was my appendage, constantly at my side and in my car (I did finally get a car too). The problem with dogs is that they do not live as long as we do, and when they leave us, they also leave a hole that nothing can fill, except an endless trail of more dogs.

And so Heidi became the icon of a lifestyle and a breeding program that has spanned more than 55 years. I have had the privilege of being involved with a first-class police K-9 program, of seeing firsthand the heroism, intelligence, and courage of these wonderful animals. I have seen many from our litters go on to become guide dogs, police K-9 dogs, therapy dogs, and search-and-rescue stars, and fill a variety of other jobs in service to humanity. We have been fortunate in breeding and showing some of the finest specimens in the conformation ring and have felt the exhilaration of having the judges point to our dogs and say, "Number one!" I am proud to be associated with the breed and with the people who are dedicated to the health and improvement of the breed. I shall never be lonely, never without comfort, and never friendless as long as I am able to have a German Shepherd at my side.

The German Shepherd is not for everyone, but if you have the intelligence to stay ahead of him and the physical ability to tend to his need for a job and training, you will be rewarded with love and devotion unlike anything you have experienced in your life. If you do choose a German Shepherd, then welcome to my world! You're in for quite a ride!

David Fritsche

Chapter One

All About German Shepherds

The All-Around Servant

It has been said that the German Shepherd is first in nothing but second in everything. This simple statement sets this breed apart from all others in describing the breadth of uses of the German Shepherd. He has distinguished himself as a herding dog, police dog, search-and-rescue expert, drug detection dog, cadaver dog, therapy dog, guide dog, explosive-detection dog, and many more. Of course, first and foremost, the German Shepherd is a great family dog and companion, usually attaching himself to one person in his family or *pack*.

His many uses speak of his adaptable temperament, high degree of intelligence, and sensitive nose. The German Shepherd is a dog for all reasons, but loves to have a job and to have appreciation for a job well done.

Living with a German Shepherd can be highly rewarding or very frustrating, depending on the place he holds in the family. He is a pack animal and enjoys a role in the family, his pack. The frustration may come from the dog's not having a job and recognition for it, and of his having to create one for himself. Long periods of confinement and the absence of his pack are not good for the German Shepherd. He will find an outlet for his creative mind and energy if ignored. If he cannot protect the family, he may opt to get out and protect the entire neighborhood. He needs to be active, involved, and part of an ongoing social enterprise.

The German Shepherd is territorial, and once he has established his territory, he will guard it from intruders with his life. The task of the owner is to define that territory for him so he is free to be of service rather than being a threat to the community. He will also need to know who the alpha pack leader is. When there is a vacuum of authority in the pack, he will move into that role and assume the leadership. It is not good for the German Shepherd to be the family leader. He will prefer a submissive role and will better serve the family and the community from that subordinate status. We will deal with training in a later chapter, but gaining his submission is not hard and should never involve violence and anger. He wants a leader and will readily submit to the love of a strong and loving master. His leadership should be within his canine world, never over his human master.

If not given leadership, he may assume that role himself and do so to his own detriment. An outgoing and strong German Shepherd is a delight when in the charge of a strong and loving owner. But he should never be ignored as a simple backyard ornament or left to his own devices. He will benefit and be at his best when well trained and when he honors his owner as his alpha master.

The Herding Dog

The American Kennel Club classifies dogs in groups. One of those groups is the Herding Dogs. The German Shepherd was developed with herding as its primary assignment. The German Shepherd will herd by nature. He will herd sheep, ducks, children, or you if, in his mind, you need direction. Some of the most heroic exploits of this breed have come because of his need to protect and to move his charge out of the way of danger. It is this innate ability of the breed that makes him ideal for many of the assignments he has been given in history.

There is something awe inspiring about watching the German Shepherd in the open field, tending sheep. His long and smooth gait provides him with the ability to move easily all day long, doing the task assigned. His commanding presence is noteworthy as he takes charge of his job and does it with excitement and pride.

It has been said that the German Shepherd has "the look of eagles, which is difficult to describe but unmistakable when present." This is an apt description of the German Shepherd when he is focused on his job and enjoying his challenge.

Consider these questions before you purchase a German Shepherd:

1. Can you provide the exercise that is essential for a herding dog who wants to do something productive—a job?

2. Can you provide the training that will make your German Shepherd a productive member of the community rather than a nuisance?

3. Do you have the time and the will to stay on top of an intelligent animal who is smarter than most of your friends?

4. Do you have a yard with a fence at least 6 feet high (1.8 m) with enough room for him to work?

5. Are you strong enough to be the alpha of the pack, yet gentle enough to be the loving leader?

German Shepherd Beginnings

The German Shepherd is a relatively new breed going back just over 100 years. Whereas some dog breeds date back to ancient Egypt or prehistory, the German Shepherd's history dates only to just before the turn of the twentieth century.

In the mid- to late 1800s in Europe, there was an attempt to standardize dog breeds and to secure the traits for which they were bred. In 1891 the Phylax Society was formed in Germany with the stated goal of standardizing dog breeds. Although the group lasted only a few short years, it did provide the inspiration for many breeds to begin the process of standardization and for other breeds to be developed. It was in this period that an ex-cavalry captain, Max von Stephanitz, began his work to create a superior herding dog. In 1899, Captin Max attended a dog show and was attracted to a dog named Hektor Linksrhein. He was so taken with the intelligence and working abilities of this dog that he purchased him and changed his name to Horand von Grafrath. He then founded the Verein fur Schaferhunde (the Society for German Shepherds) and Horand became the first registered dog in the society and the father of the breed.

The breed grew in popularity in Germany and other parts of Europe, but did not get a firm foothold in the United States until later. In 1913 the German Shepherd Club of America was formed and became the recognized breed club of the American Kennel Club.

The breed was not as popular as it is today until Hollywood entered the scene, popularizing the breed with movies starring Strongheart and Rin Tin Tin. The popularity of the breed in military service in World War I provided the backdrop for the Hollywood stars who followed, and soon, the breed

Helpful Hints

Did You Know

There were more than 26 Rin Tin Tin Warner Brothers movies, played by more than five Rin Tin Tin progeny. Before the first film, Warner Brothers was facing bankruptcy. This German Shepherd not only saved lives in the film but saved the company.

At the peak of his career, he received more than 10,000 fan letters a week.

was on its way to long-term popularity. Records from dog registries around the world show the German Shepherd in one of the top three spots in popularity since the breed became popular in the mid-1900s, making it the most popular breed overall in the world since that time.

The Many Jobs of the German Shepherd

In addition to the traditional jobs done by the German Shepherd, there are some interesting developments in the breadth of the breed's use. During the rescue efforts at the World Trade Center after the terrorist attack on September 11, 2001, the German Shepherd was the dominant breed on-site and contributed many heroic efforts, including the shortening of the rescue process. It was estimated that one German Shepherd could do the work of a dozen human search members because of their scenting ability and knack for the task. He is simply more efficient with some tasks than his human counterparts. One of those tasks is search and rescue. A national net-

work of search-and-rescue clubs has sprung up across the nation whose sole purpose is to assist communities and police organizations in finding missing and lost people. They usually include cadaver dog training for any of the club members who want to pursue that specialty. Although other breeds are also used, the German Shepherd is still, as always, the predominant breed of choice.

Experiments are also being conducted on the medical use of the German Shepherd. While animal jokes proliferate on the Internet about "cat scans" and "lab reports," animals are actually making inroads into medical diagnostics. The scenting ability of dogs allows them to identify scents that we humans simply cannot smell.

"Dr. Armand Cognetta of Tallahassee, FL, an expert in melanomas, began researching if dogs could detect skin cancer. He enlisted the help of a dog trainer, and with samples of melanomas tried to train dogs to sniff out skin cancer. George, the dog used in the study, was able to detect the melanoma 99% of the time" (report from *SiriusDog.com*).

Breed Truths

It is common to hear people talk about the Alsatian and the Police Dog as separate breeds from the German Shepherd. The confusion comes from the English change of the breed's name during World War I to Alsatian and the popular use of the breed in police work, leading to the misnomer "Police Dog" referring to a breed.

Both of these designations are misnomers of the German Shepherd.

German Shepherds' use with people with disabilities is legend. They were the breed of choice for many years in the Guide Dogs for the Blind program and have been used as hearing dogs, therapy dogs in hospitals, and for children with disabilities, and for those needing a helping hand or a listening ear. This great dog has been involved in so many applications of service to humanity that it is difficult to document them all. He has been the hunter, protector, herder, and friend. He is adaptable to be anything we train him to be and more. He is an extension of our human hand and heart in doing with us and for us anything we need done.

Breed Truths

Loyalty . . .

The German Shepherd is an extremely loyal dog. He will bond with a family and with one particular member of the family as his primary master and will give his life to protect his charge.

This virtue is one of the chief reasons for his use in military and police service, along with his keen intellect and ability to distinguish between the general social interaction of the humans around him and the contrast of criminal or threatening activity by an enemy.

His keen sense of smell, intelligence, and loyalty make him an ideal working partner in many tasks.

The German Shepherd has been successfully used to search out land mines by various countries and also in civil conflicts in Africa. Traditional land-mine search techniques had involved the use of metal detectors until Vernon Joynt, a trainer and handler in South Africa, popularized the use of the German Shepherd. Modern explosive mines contain very little metal and the explosive material has changed, so former detection methods do not work. The phenolic resin–based explosives, however, did not escape the nose of the German Shepherd, who quickly became legend in his ability to detect and communicate the location of the mines.

German Shepherds have also distinguished themselves as fire dogs and investigators of arson. They have been trained to detect the smells of petrochemicals in the prevention of unsafe and fire-prone sites and also to detect the presence of accelerants at fire scenes.

In fact the German Shepherd has been used to detect certain minerals, contaminated foodstuffs, cancer, diabetes, allergens, mycrotoxins, termites, the feces trails of wild animals, pollutants, counterfeit currency, truffles, and more. He is truly an amazing animal with an unparalleled record of service to mankind.

Although the history of the German Shepherd is easily traceable in his service to humanity in the civil duties he is called upon to perform as well as his use in police work and the military, there are some dark clouds on the horizon in recent days. The rash of breed-specific legislation that has become popular in recent years finds some political jurisdictions naming the German Shepherd as a dangerous breed. Declining registration figures for all breeds, including the German Shepherd, because of anti-breeding and breed-specific

FYI: The BIG Dog Craze

Although the German Shepherd standard calls for a medium-sized dog (females 22–24 inches at the shoulder and males 24–26 inches) some breeders have bred for size alone and have produced dogs that are labeled as giant, large old style, extra large, and other adjectives that ignore the standard and also ignore the structural integrity of the breed.

Although each litter will have a variation in sizes within the litter, ignoring the standard and the structural health issues of the breed is frowned upon by the breed club, the German Shepherd Club of America, and oversized dogs are not permitted in many foreign registries.

legislation, may find our reliance on this breed altered in the future. Is it possible that the day is just ahead of us when the history of service of this great breed is forgotten in the push of those who propose to eliminate pets from our world and stop all breeding?

As our culture shifts from a generally rural and agricultural base to a more cosmopolitan setting where dogs are not an asset but a liability, we may find the development of an antagonistic atmosphere toward this great breed that has so selflessly served us for more than 100 years. That would be both unfortunate and unacceptable for those who know this breed and love it. It would also be a disaster for those who need him in the services he provides to humanity.

The German Shepherd Timeline

1891: Phylax Society is formed in Germany for defining and preserving dog breeds.

1899: Max von Stephanitz forms the S.V.—German Shepherd Registry.

1899: SV holds first "Sieger" dog show.

1906: First German Shepherd sets foot (paw) on American soil.

1907: First German Shepherd exhibited in America.

1908: First German Shepherd accepted by AKC registry.

1908: First German Shepherd arrives in British Isles.

1913: German Shepherd Dog Club of America is formed.

1913: First AKC Championship awarded to a German Shepherd.

1914: German Shepherds distinguish the breed in World War I.

1915: First GSDCA National Specialty Show in Greenwich, CT.

1917: During the war with Germany, the AKC changed the German Shepherd's name to the Shepherd Dog and England changes it to the Alsatian.

1921: Strongheart, a German Shepherd, becomes a movie star, increasing the breed's popularity.

1923: Rin Tin Tin becomes a film star, making 26 feature films.

1925: The titles of Grand Victor and Grand Victrix are given to the first-place male and female select dogs at the GSDCA National Specialty Show.

1933: The German Shepherd becomes the third most popular breed in the AKC registry (in just 25 years) and has been in the top four ever since.

1936: Captain Max von Stephanitz, the founder of the German Shepherd and author of the GSD Standard, dies in Germany.

1977: The name of the breed is changed back to the German Shepherd in America, Australia, and several other countries after having been renamed to Alsatian during WWI.

The German Shepherd Standard

Each recognized dog breed has a standard that comes from its original breed club and is accepted by a breed registry. The largest breed registry in America is the American Kennel Club (AKC). The breed standard is developed not by the AKC but by the recognized breed club, in this case, the German Shepherd Dog Club of America (GSDCA). The AKC and other registries recognize a "parent" club, which is the breed club that holds in trust the standard and sets policy for the regional clubs in their breed activities and AKC-recognized sporting events.

Fun Facts

Shortly after WWI the German Shepherd became the most popular dog in Germany, in just a few short years. By 1933 this breed was the third most popular breed in the United States. By the end of WWII the German Shepherd was in the top three of all breeds in all nations of the world with dog registries and remains so today. Taken as a whole, this means the German Shepherd was the most popular breed in the world within a few short years after its acceptance as a registered breed.

General Appearance

The first impression of a good German Shepherd is that of a strong, agile, well-muscled animal, alert and full of life. It is well balanced, with harmonious development of the forequarter and hindquarter. The dog is longer than tall, deep-bodied, and presents an outline of smooth curves rather than angles. It looks substantial and not spindly, giving the impression, both at rest and in motion, of muscular fitness and nimbleness without any look of clumsiness or soft living. The ideal dog is stamped with a look of quality and nobility—difficult to define, but unmistakable when present. Secondary sex characteristics are strongly marked, and every animal gives a definite impression of masculinity or femininity, according to its sex.

Temperament

The breed has a distinct personality marked by direct and fearless, but not hostile, expression, self-confidence and a certain aloofness that does not lend itself to immediate and indiscrimi-

nate friendships. The dog must be approachable, quietly standing his ground and showing confidence and willingness to meet overtures without himself making them. He is poised, but when the occasion demands, eager and alert; both fit and willing to serve in his capacity as companion, watchdog, blind leader, herding dog, or guardian, whichever the circumstances may demand. The dog must not be timid, shrinking behind his master or handler; he should not be nervous, looking about or upward with anxious expression or showing nervous reactions, such as tucking of tail, to strange sounds or sights. Lack of confidence under any surroundings is not typical of good character. Any of the above deficiencies in character which indicate shyness must be penalized as very serious faults and any dog exhibiting pronounced indications of these must be excused from the ring. Any dog that attempts to bite the judge must be disqualified. The ideal dog is a working animal with an incorruptible character combined with body and gait suitable for the arduous work that constitutes his primary purpose.

Size, Proportion, Substance
The desired height for males at the top of the highest point of the shoulder blade is 24 to 26 inches; and for bitches, 22 to 24 inches.

The German Shepherd is longer than tall, with the most desirable proportion as 10 to 8½. The length is measured from the point of the prosternum or breastbone to the rear edge of the pelvis, the ischial tuberosity. The desirable long proportion is not derived from a long back, but from overall length with relation to height, which is achieved by length of forequarter and length of withers and hindquarter, viewed from the side.

Head

The head is noble, cleanly chiseled, strong without coarseness, but above all not fine, and in proportion to the body. The head of the male is distinctly masculine, and that of the bitch distinctly feminine.

The expression is keen, intelligent, and composed. Eyes are of medium size, almond shaped, set a little obliquely and not protruding. The color is as dark as possible. Ears are moderately pointed, in proportion to the skull, open toward the front, and carried erect when at attention, the ideal carriage being one in which the center lines of the ears, viewed from the front, are parallel to each other and perpendicular to the ground. A dog with cropped or hanging ears must be disqualified.

Seen from the front the forehead is only moderately arched, and the skull slopes into the long, wedge-shaped muzzle without abrupt stop. The muzzle is long and strong, and its topline is parallel to the topline of the skull. Nose is black. A dog with a nose that is not predominantly black must be disqualified. The lips are firmly fitted. Jaws are strongly developed. Teeth—42 in number—20 upper and 22 lower—are strongly developed and meet in a scissors bite in which part of the inner surface of the upper incisors meet and engage part of the outer surface of the lower incisors. An overshot jaw or a level bite is undesirable. An undershot jaw is a disqualifying fault. Complete dentition is to be preferred. Any missing teeth other than first premolars is a serious fault.

Neck, Topline, Body

The neck is strong and muscular, clean-cut and relatively long, proportionate in size to the head, and without loose folds of skin. When the dog is at attention or excited, the head is raised and the neck carried high; otherwise typical carriage of the head is forward rather than up and but little higher than the top of the shoulders, particularly in motion.

Topline The withers are higher than and sloping into the level back. The back is straight, very strongly developed without sag or roach, and relatively short. The whole structure of the body gives an impression of depth and solidity without bulkiness.

Chest Commencing at the prosternum, it is well filled and carried well down between the legs. It is deep and capacious, never shallow, with ample room for lungs and heart, carried well forward, with the prosternum showing ahead of the shoulder in profile. Ribs well sprung and long, neither barrel-shaped nor too flat, and carried down to a sternum which reaches to the elbows. Correct ribbing allows the elbows to move back freely when the dog is at a trot. Too round causes interference and throws the elbows out; too flat or short causes pinched elbows. Ribbing is carried well back so that the loin is relatively short. Abdomen is firmly held and not paunchy. The bottom line is only moderately tucked up in the loin.

Loin Viewed from the top, broad and strong. Undue length between the last rib and the thigh, when viewed from the side, is undesirable. Croup is long and gradually sloping.

Tail bushy, with the last vertebra extended at least to the hock joint. It is set smoothly into the croup and low rather than high. At rest, the tail hangs in a slight curve like a saber. A slight hook— sometimes carried to one side—is faulty only to the extent that it mars general appearance. When the dog is excited or in motion, the curve is accentuated and the tail raised, but it should never be curled forward beyond a vertical line. Tails too short, or with clumpy ends due to ankylosis, are serious faults. A dog with a docked tail must be disqualified.

Forequarters

The shoulder blades are long and obliquely angled, laid on flat and not placed forward. The upper arm joins the shoulder blade at about a right angle. Both the upper arm and the shoulder blade are well muscled. The forelegs, viewed from all sides, are straight and the bone oval rather than round. The pasterns are strong and springy and angulated at approximately a 25-degree angle from the vertical. Dewclaws on the forelegs may be removed, but are normally left on.

The feet are short, compact with toes well arched, pads thick and firm, nails short and dark.

Hindquarters

The whole assembly of the thigh, viewed from the side, is broad, with both upper and lower thigh well muscled, forming as nearly as possible a right angle. The upper thigh bone parallels the shoulder blade while the lower thigh bone parallels the upper arm. The metatarsus (the unit between the hock joint and the foot) is short, strong, and tightly articulated. The dewclaws, if any, should be removed from the hind legs.

Fun Facts

The German Shepherd and Politics

The German Shepherd has also made it into politics, having been companions to Presidents John Kennedy, Calvin Coolidge, Herbert Hoover, and Franklin D. Roosevelt, and to Vice President Joe Biden.

This does not, however, give us a picture of the true political leaning of the breed. He may be non-partisan.

Coat

The ideal dog has a double coat of medium length. The outer coat should be as dense as possible, hair straight, harsh, and lying close to the body. A slightly wavy outer coat, often of wiry texture, is permissible. The head, including the inner ear and foreface, and the legs and paws are covered with short hair, and the neck with longer and thicker hair. The rear of the forelegs and hind legs has somewhat longer hair extending to the pastern and hock, respectively. Faults in coat include soft, silky, too long outer coat, woolly, curly, and open coat

Color

The German Shepherd varies in color, and most colors are permissible. Strong rich colors are preferred. Pale, washed-out colors and blues or livers are serious faults. A white dog must be disqualified.

Gait

A German Shepherd is a trotting dog, and its structure has been developed to meet the requirements of its work. General Impression—The gait is out-reaching, elastic, seemingly without effort, smooth and rhythmic, covering the maximum amount of ground with the minimum number of steps. At a

walk it covers a great deal of ground, with long stride of both hind legs and forelegs. At a trot the dog covers still more ground with even longer stride, and moves powerfully but easily, with coordination and balance so that the gait appears to be the steady motion of a well-lubricated machine. The feet travel close to the ground on both forward reach and backward push. In order to achieve ideal movement of this kind, there must be good muscular development and ligamentation. The hindquarters deliver, through the back, a powerful forward thrust which slightly lifts the whole animal and drives the body forward. Reaching far under, and passing the imprint left by the front foot, the hind foot takes hold of the ground; then hock, stifle, and upper thigh come into play and sweep back, the stroke of the hind leg finishing with the foot still close to the ground in a smooth follow-through. The over-reach of the hindquarter usually necessitates one hind foot passing outside and the other hind foot passing inside the track of the forefeet, and such action is not faulty unless the locomotion is crabwise with the dog's body sideways out of the normal straight line.

Transmission

The typical smooth, flowing gait is maintained with great strength and firmness of back. The whole effort of the hindquarter is transmitted to the forequarter through the loin, back, and withers. At full trot, the back must remain firm and level without sway, roll, whip, or roach. Unlevel topline with withers lower than the hip is a fault. To compensate for the forward motion imparted by the hindquarters, the shoulder should open to its full extent. The forelegs should reach out close to the ground in a long stride in harmony with that of the hindquarters. The dog does not track on widely separated parallel lines, but brings the feet inward toward the middle line of the body when trotting, in order to maintain balance. The feet track closely but do not strike or cross over. Viewed from the front, the front legs function from the shoulder joint to the pad in a straight line. Viewed from the rear, the hind legs function from the hip joint to the pad in a straight line. Faults of gait, whether from front, rear, or side, are to be considered very serious faults.

Disqualifications

- **Cropped or hanging ears.**
- **Dogs with noses not predominantly black.**
- **Undershot jaw.**
- **Docked tail.**
- **White dogs.**
- **Any dog that attempts to bite the judge**.

Breed Truths

During World War II, the German Snow Troops used all-white German Shepherds to blend into the snow-covered landscape. They also wore all-white field uniforms, making them famous for their surprise attacks. These were some of the most feared enemies of the Allied Forces.

The GSDCA Standard was an exact copy of the World Union of German Shepherd Dog Associations (WUSV) standard when the club began, simply a translation from the German language to English. But over the years slight changes have been made in both standards, making them slightly different in wording. The above American standard was approved February 11, 1978, and was then reformatted on July 11, 1994, emphasizing temperament by moving that section of the standard to the top of the list of standard items.

Conversely, the German standard has changed far more often in that their system has a different governmental form in which the president has greater influence and, in some cases, lifetime tenure. Most of those presidents have influenced changes in the standard. Whether this is good or bad is a matter of opinion and discussion, yet there are those in both systems of government who propose that their standard is more pure and thus better.

To understand the standard one has to understand that it is weighted. That is, not all faults are equal in value. Although the disqualifying faults are listed as such, other faults are in the descriptive language of the standard. An easy way to view the standard is as follows:

Preferences are those items that are not listed as a fault but are described as desirable or to be preferred. They include dark, rich colors, a complete set of teeth, and any other item that is not specified as a fault.

Faults are items that are specifically indicated as faults and are more serious than mere preferences but not as serious as those to follow.

Serious Faults are enumerated, including missing teeth, other than missing first pre-molars, which are listed after the mention that a "full dentition is preferred" (a preference). There are a number of serious faults such as pale, washed-out colors, blues and liver colors, short tails, and others.

Very Serious Faults There are only a few very serious faults. One is a fault of temperament and the other is any fault of movement. From this comes the question most asked by judges: Can this dog do what he was bred to do all day without tiring? The long, easy, ground-covering gait of the German Shepherd is a primary characteristic. The movement of both front and rear leg assemblies should be long, extended, and smooth, showing coordinated strides without giving the body an up-and-down motion as is typical of other breeds. The German Shepherd should appear suspended in the air, moving forward easily, without a flurry of steps or vertical motion.

Disqualifications are innumerate in the standard. One of the great controversies in the breed is the issue of the White German Shepherd. The white coat color was listed as a disqualifying color in Germany in 1933. In 1959 the GSDCA standard was again made to conform to the German Standard, which eliminated the white color from conformation competition. In 1968 the AKC affirmed the disqualification of the white coat color. Today, the German Shepherd may be AKC registered regardless of color and may compete in performance events. He is disqualified only from conformation competition.

White German Shepherd enthusiasts have formed their own breed club, the American White Shepherd Association, and enjoy competing with exclusively white-coated dogs.

Fun Facts

German Shepherds have the largest number of organized clubs, training organizations, and events of any breed.

It is said that all dogs have some faults and there is no perfect dog. It might also be said there are no perfect judges, which is why the AKC requires that a dog earning the title of Champion earn those points from three different judges and have two major show wins. A major show is one in which the number of dogs is large enough to warrant the winning of three or more points from the point schedule. This is designed to level out the possibilities of both imperfections of biases in judging and in the dogs themselves. To obtain the title of Champion, a dog must earn 15 points at AKC-approved shows. Other registries have similar point requirements, and some require fewer points.

10 **Questions** About German Shepherds

1 **Do German Shepherds need a fenced yard?**

Absolutely! The German Shepherd is very intelligent and hence is very inquisitive. He needs an outlet for that need to move about and explore, and without confinement will do so with or without your permission. He is also primarily territorial and needs his territory defined. Unless it is defined for him, he will expand his territory until he owns the entire neighborhood. A good fence is good for the German Shepherd.

2 **Do German Shepherds shed?**

Yes, they do. He will shed seasonally based on the weather zone in which you live, usually just before spring, again in the summer, and just before winter. The female German Shepherd will also shed just before she comes into heat if she is not spayed. It is hard to predict exactly when the shedding will start, but you will know when it comes. Grooming during this time is good for him and is also a great time for bonding. He will learn to love his grooming.

3 **Are German Shepherds hyperactive?**

No! Some import lines are bred for "high drive" and personal protection sports, and they can be more active than other lines that are not bred for this purpose. Check with your breeder to make sure you are getting what you are after. Most German Shepherds make great house dogs, and although they need training and directed activities, they will fall into family routines and can lie down and rest with the family.

4 **Are German Shepherds difficult to housetrain?**

No, not at all. The biggest issue in housetraining is getting the owner to be aware of the signs that he needs to go out. He will give signals—sniffing the floor, walking about aimlessly, and perhaps even going to the door to get your attention. The easiest way to housetrain is to let him sleep in a dog crate and as soon as he awakes, let him out. He is a den animal and will love his crate. Then simply learn his signals and watch for them. The German Shepherd is among the easiest of all breeds to housetrain.

5 **Are German Shepherds hard to obedience-train?**

No, they are among the easiest to train. Most obedience trainers will say that the hardest thing to do is train the owners how to tell him what to do. Find a good program in your area or read some good training books and your German Shepherd will help you learn to train him.

6 **Is the German Shepherd good with kids?**

Yes, very good. The German Shepherd intuitively loves babies and children. He understands "little people" and seems to prefer them sometimes. He is a great family dog and will herd the children to safety and protect them from outsiders. But a word of caution: Once bonded with the family, he can become overly protective of the children if not guided and supervised.

7 How often should I bathe my German Shepherd?

Dogs do not have sweat glands as humans do, and cool themselves by panting—breathing in cool air and exhaling hot air. So, his body does not need cleansing as often as ours does. The hair of the German Shepherd lies flat, so it is usually not easily matted. This breed has been called "the wash-and-wear dog." It is not necessary to bathe the German Shepherd more than once a month or when he has gotten himself into something smelly. If you smell him, bathe him; otherwise just love him.

8 Do I have to exercise my German Shepherd every day?

Yes! If you don't, he will either exercise himself or become fat, lazy, and mentally dull. He lives to move and do things. He delights to explore and learn. He will love to go for a walk or a ride, but will excel at some disciplined activity like agility, obedience, herding, tracking, or any other organized activity.

9 Is the German Shepherd a dangerous breed?

It should not be! Although some political jurisdictions have labeled the German Shepherd as a dangerous breed, he has also distinguished himself as the most useful breed to mankind. Unfortunately, some people have bred for aggression, thinking that the dog should be mean to be protective. This is a terrible error that has caused untold damage to the breed. Properly bred, the German Shepherd will be protective while also being thoughtful and a good citizen. Choose your breeder carefully and select only those dogs bred for proper temperament.

10 Do German Shepherds have bad hips?

It depends! Of all breeds of dogs, German Shepherds used to be in the top three each year for incidents of hip dysplasia. Since the advent of OFA (Orthopedic Foundation for Animals) and the screening and rating of hips in dogs, the incidents have been dramatically reduced. Although all breeds have reduced their incidents of dysplasia, the German Shepherd is now down to 39th place. This is no longer the major health problem in the breed. It is part of the genetic history of the breed, however, so be sure that your breeder uses the OFA certification system or the German "A" stamp. Significant progress has been made by reputable breeders, but it is worth noting that there are breeders who are less than reputable or well meaning but ignorant of this problem who still do not use OFA certification and contribute the majority of the hip dysplasia in the breed.

Chapter Two

The Mind of the German Shepherd

The American Kennel Club lists 150 breeds of dogs in its registry. In addition, there are far more breeds listed in a variety of rare-breed registries around the world. Yet, despite all of the proliferation of dog breeds, the German Shepherd is consistently ranked in the top three for intelligence.

The challenge this represents is in being smarter than your dog. Trying to figure out what is going on inside his head will keep the German Shepherd owner busy and either delighted or frustrated, depending on what you want in a dog. This breed is not for the faint of heart or the lazy in body. The dog's activity is seldom aimless, but generated by some plan and grand purpose. His mind is actively thinking and interpreting his world and deciding how to enjoy it and conquer it. This is not a mentally lazy dog but a breed with extremely high intellect and a breadth of application for that intelligence.

This chapter is dedicated to helping you find some keys to both understanding your German Shepherd and leading him into the productive life he desires and of which he is capable.

Understanding the German Shepherd Mind

Many clinical articles have been written about dogs, concluding that they are simply recipients of external stimuli, acting only on given situations and their basic animal instincts. In other words, they do not think; they only respond. Dogs in this theory are said to be subject to human anthropomorphism—the assignment of human characteristics. Such information certainly did not come from anyone who has lived with a German Shepherd. The motivation of this great dog is to actively participate in the world of the pack. He needs to be part of the activities of the family and to have a useful job to do. If he is not challenged, he will discover activities that satisfy his need for a challenge and for mental and physical stimulation without supervision. He needs to explore his world and to discover how it works. He is bright,

FYI: What About K-9 Dogs?

Although police K-9 dogs were predominately German Shepherds from the 1930s through the 1980s, several other breeds have come to be used as well. The separation of work roles in police K-9 work made way for specialties such as drug dogs, search-and-rescue dogs, bomb dogs, and so forth. Other breeds with keen noses who are less intimidating than the German Shepherd are used for various purposes, but the German Shepherd is still the predominate breed, and for all-around use, is usually the breed of choice.

Contrary to some rumors, police K-9 dogs are not trained to kill, but to bite and hold a violent suspect until ordered to release by the handler. These same dogs are also used to search for missing children and to do presentations in public places and schools. For the dog, a focused play drive is what they use in police service. Mean dogs do not make it in the police K-9 world.

curious, and brave in exploring his immediate territory and beyond. He thinks, decides, and plans.

To understand the German Shepherd mind is to press beyond the limits of our relationship to things and most animals and to be faced with a formidable challenge. Here is an animal, unlike most on the planet, who is far more like humans than any other, who has the ability to reason, plan, structure, and execute those plans and structures. For this reason and more, it is said that the owner of a German Shepherd should be at least as smart as the dog.

The territorial nature of the German Shepherd will drive him to explore his yard, but also to venture beyond, in search of information about his world. Social by nature, he will find a pack, and will most often be the pack leader if not guided into a subordinate position. If you doubt who owns the world, just ask him. He'll most likely tell you—"It is I."

Once secure in a family pack, he will live and die to protect his pack and to nurture those under his care. His social needs are usually met in the confines of one family, and he couldn't care less about everyone else in the world. The standard for the breeds calls him "aloof." It is not that he does not like other people or dogs as much as it is his nature to have a primary attachment to the pack and particularly one person in the pack. His brain is hardwired to be loyal, protective, and giving. His life is not defined by individualism but by his identity and place in the pack. The "aloof" nature will make him seem unfriendly to some, and they are right. He is not necessarily aggressive without provocation, but is aloof in that he does not need approval or friendship outside his pack or family. He is secure in having a few close friends in a world in which the rest do not matter.

Once bonded to his family and usually to one particular person in that family, he will be content to live out his life in service to them and will sacrifice his own life if necessary to protect them.

A Mind to Work

The German Shepherd has a desire to be useful and delights in the mental stimulation of learning and developing skills that are productive. Bred to herd, the tending nature is always there, ready to find a means of expression. Jobs such as police work, tracking, guiding, protection, drug detection, military operations, and security are natural places for the German Shepherd, but he will also excel at herding sheep, ducks, and cattle, or just working around the farm.

Competition trials and dog shows are also a delight to the German Shepherd. Adept at obedience trials, which are the basis for many other dog competitions, he loves to please his master, needing praise and love above all, although an occasional treat doesn't hurt. Agility, tracking, schutzhund (obedience, tracking, and personal protection), and any other competitive activity will stimulate his mind and fulfill his need to be active and useful. In the grandeur of the conformation ring, he will know when he wins and when he loses and will even sulk if he did not do well. He loves to be with his people and to win their approval. Give him a job and you give him a life.

The dominance of German Shepherds searching the rubble after the bombing of the Twin Towers in New York after September 11, 2001, is a testimony to the usefulness of this great breed. When the stories of heroic rescues and saving of lives are told, it is most often a German Shepherd who is the star. Whether it is a bombing, flood, avalanche, or other disaster, they are mankind's first choice for a canine worker.

PERSONALITY POINTERS
German Shepherd Body Language

German Shepherd Mood	Friendly	Interested or Excited	Playful
Head Carriage	Normal posture	Neck extended, head forward	Bowing or moving side to side
Eyes	Normal	Wide, focused in stare	Bright and opened
Ears	Normal, erect	Erect, rotated forward	May move back slightly, erect
Mouth	Open, tongue hanging out	Closed, sniffing	Open, may be "talking"
Body	Relaxed, normal	Flexed muscles, rear feet positioned like sprinter	Flexed muscles, may dance from side to side
Tail	May wag or remain normal	May swish, but moved down like a rudder	Wagging

Around the House

The towels are missing from the bathroom, as is the toilet paper roll. The books have been rearranged, and there is a hole in the backyard flower bed. The back door is open and the cat got out. All these and more are signs that your German Shepherd is bored and thinking of things to do. He will steal your clothes to cover his bed, chew on your shoe, and, after stealing the remote control, change channels on the TV. He is capable of so many different things because he is a thinker. He will probably not exhibit aimless nervous energy as some dogs do, but he will work out complex schemes in his head and then carry them out with some amazing results. It is for this reason that your German Shepherd will need a regular routine of work and exercise. He is capable of waiting for it, if he is assured it is coming. The schedule is in his mind, and he knows when it is time to get up, to go for a walk, or to do the chore that is his. He will not forget, for that is the height of his day.

Once the routine is established and he knows he will have his regular fun times with his master and the family, then he is usually not destructive. It is

Apprehensive or Anxious	Submissive	Fearful	Dominant
Tongue retracted; head pulled back	Normal posture	Head slightly down, snarl or bark	Neck extended, head high, may put head over other dog's neck
Narrowed, focused	Lowered, looking away or down	Narrowed, focused	Wide, bright
Rotated forward, may lie back slightly	Folded back, "taco ear"	Erect, rotated forward	Erect, forward
Closed	Closed	Barking, snarling	Open, tongue out
Tensed, flexed, ready to move	Relaxed or may lie down or roll onto back	Tensed, flexed, ready to move	"Parading" or strutting
May swish, but moved down like a rudder	Wagging	Down, but seldom between legs	Up, may curl slightly upward

best, however, to keep the trash, shoes, and toilet paper out of reach, or at least out of sight.

A Broad-Minded Thinker

The German Shepherd has a broad range of attributes that makes him the generalist of many uses. He may not have the scenting ability of some of the hound breeds, but he is widely used for that purpose because of the combination of other attributes that make him the overall broad-minded thinker. He will know, with training, what to do with the information his brain receives.

All of the German Shepherd senses—smell, hearing, eyesight—are much more acute than ours. His world does not have the same limits that ours does. He is therefore useful to us in many ways, if we but learn how he perceives his world and what his true abilities are. It is well to learn to trust him in areas where his senses are more acute than ours, including many times, his perception of people.

Danger Ahead

The German Shepherd is smart, with keen senses and a sensitive nature, but he can also be dangerous without proper training and supervision. His protective nature and territorial instincts can make him less than social, and without training and control, he may bite people or other animals. His instinct predisposes him to look at his world to find the threat and deal with it. He will most often be able to distinguish between the real threat and the unthreatening visitor. But without the human presence to guide that development and to socialize him, he can easily become overly aggressive when he perceives his territory is invaded.

Socialization and training are the essential ingredients in directing his natural instincts into a more thoughtful pattern of behavior. It is unfortunate that the German Shepherd is involved in a disproportionate number of bite incidents. It is almost never toward the family but in protection of his family and territory. Directing those instincts is essential to having a good citizen. Not everyone should own a German Shepherd. Those who decide to should dedicate their time and energy to challenge him to be a good citizen with proper socialization and training.

The Need for Order

There is a peculiar thing about most German Shepherds: They want things in order. Although it is probably a genetic trait, it is definitely present in the breed. Your dog will think in boxes and straight lines. He will appreciate a clean bed, and although he will play in the mud, he will want to be groomed properly afterward. You might discover that he reacts to disorder and to changing the familiar patterns of things. He will not like the furniture rearranged or someone else in his place. Everyone should have a place and not mix things up too frequently. Discovering his need for order can be quite comical.

This sense of order is also hierarchical with the pack. The alpha dog will see that the other dogs do what is "right" and will discipline those who violate the order of things. He may even straighten up after you from time to time. You will also note, if you have multiple dogs, that if you call one who does not respond, the alpha dog will discipline him when he finally does for not responding quickly. This reinforced order is usually a bump or a soft mouth over his neck, but it is clearly an order to be obeyed.

The German Shepherd will also notice things about people that are unusual. If a person has an uncommon hat, a backpack, or some other offbeat clothing or object, he will alert to it and be on guard.

This sense of order also translates into the right place for his activities. He will want to eat in the same place, sleep in his place, and be with the family in a certain place. Somewhere in the German Shepherd brain is an organizational chart that needs to be obeyed.

COMPATIBILITY Is a German Shepherd the Best Breed for You?

ENERGY LEVEL MODERATE, NOT AIMLESS	• • •
EXERCISE REQUIREMENTS – DAILY	• • • •
PLAYFULNESS – LOVES FUN AND GAMES	• • • •
AFFECTION LEVEL – A LOVER	• • • •
FRIENDLINESS TOWARD OTHER PETS – NOT STRANGE PETS	•
FRIENDLINESS TOWARD STRANGERS ON GUARD	•
FRIENDLINESS TOWARD CHILDREN – IF KNOWN	• • •
EASE OF TRAINING – VERY EASY	• • • •
GROOMING EFFORT – NOT MUCH REQUIRED	•
SHEDDING – OH,YES	• • •
SPACE REQUIREMENT – NEEDS SPACE	• • •
OK FOR BEGINNERS—USUALLY GREAT	• • •

4 Dots = Highest rating on scale

Reading the German Shepherd Mind

You will be able soon enough to watch the body language and facial expressions and read his mind. But rest assured that he will also soon be able to watch you and read your mind, so be aware: You might be the master, but you may not always be his equal. His moods will vary from happy to tired to adventurous to playful. He will communicate those moods easily through the ears, eyes, mouth, and his posture and expressions. The more you learn to read his communications, the more you will enjoy him. He is not an inanimate object to set in a display case to be admired. He is a living creation of great beauty and value, to be honored,

Fun Facts

At age two the average child understands about 50 words, but by age three, word recognition soars to about 900.

The average dog recognizes about 150 words and the average German Shepherd more than 250.

FYI: 9/11 Hero Dogs

More than 350 dogs partnered with their human handlers in the search effort after the bombing and collapse of the Twin Towers in New York City on September 11, 2001. Labs, Golden Retrievers, Terriers, and several other breeds worked side by side with the predominant German Shepherds, saving lives and finding bodies. This may well have been the largest single deployment of dogs in history, and the results were remarkable.

Although thousands of people perished, there are no accurate figures for the number who might have died were it not for the "live find" of the rescue dogs. And the efficiency of the cadaver dogs greatly reduced the time it took to discover those who were not rescued.

These dogs are now memorialized by their own monument and volumes of books and web pages in their honor.

tended to, and cared for. The highest purpose of the German Shepherd is to love and be loved.

This breed is capable of a strong bond of love that is deep and without condition. He is forgiving and thoughtful, ever concerned for your health and welfare. His devotion will show in his play and in his resting, in his graciousness and protectiveness. You will never feed him without his returning to your location after eating to say thank you.

He is not, however, human. That is sometimes hard to understand. Yes, he is smarter than some humans, and more loyal than most, but he will remind you regularly that he is a dog.

CAUTION

Your dog will always love you and want to obey. If he does not "get it," keep trying and don't lose your temper with him. If you hit your dog, he will learn to fear your hand and you and will be confused in the process. If you are frustrated enough to lose your temper, you need retraining, not the dog!

Positive reinforcement and repetition will get the job done, and both you and the dog will be much happier. The ultimate objective of training is a relationship of love, not of fear.

He will lick where you think he shouldn't and dig and shed and do things that remind you he is a dog. His thought patterns and behavior, as amazing as they are, do not elevate him to human status. You, the owner, are still responsible for his care and behavior. You are the leader, and he wants you to be. Being strong for him does not mean being heavy-handed or abusive, but it does mean that you take the lead, give the commands, and do the training. He needs you to be the alpha of the pack.

FYI: The German Wolf Dog

A number of dog breeds are similar in appearance to the wolf with erect ears, such as the Tervueren, Groenendaej, Malinois, Bohemian Shepherd, German Shepherd, the Husky, and the Dutch Shepherd. There are even some recent hybrid dogs that are crossbred with wolves for various unknown reasons. These have all been referred to as Wolf Dogs.

The fact is, appearance does not denote a close relationship to the wolf. Some anthropologists believe all dogs are descendants of the wolf, because wolves predated humankind. Some, however, believe that the dog predates the wolf and that the wild dog species are those who because of temperament could not conform to human companionship.

Whatever the reality of prehistory, we can only theorize, but the German Shepherd is a new breed as dog breeds go, dating back just over 100 years. Although rumored to have been crossbred with wolves, von Stephanitz's exacting records of his breeding program do not leave any doubt about the purity of the breed and their origin as herding dogs from domesticated herding stock.

Play Drive and Humor

Play drive, we are told, is simply prey drive focused and disciplined. The German Shepherd, like most dogs, is a hunter, but unlike many breeds, will hunt anything that moves—rabbits, lizards, squirrels, or anything else that runs from him. The process of focusing that drive starts early in puppyhood, directing that drive to toys and other objects that are acceptable. In schutzhund training, burlap toys are used as play objects, and the trainer substitutes larger burlap toys until the dog is "on the sleeve." The "sleeve" is the burlap arm pad that is worn in the schutzhund training for bite work.

For most of us, just enjoying the play drive of the German Shepherd is enough. He is a great playmate, willing to play ball, tug-of-war, or many other games of interaction. Involved in the play you will find a sense of humor. He will delight in deceptive motions, doing the unexpected, and in general, making a fool out of his master. This

Breed Truths

Smell is the German Shepherd's dominant sense and is estimated to be 100,000 times greater than our own. He can also hear better, see better, and sense motion better than we can.

Although it is generally believed that the human has far greater reasoning ability, the German Shepherd has far more natural data to evaluate in his decision making and in relating to his world.

sense of humor betrays his high degree of intelligence and also is a delightful trait to be around. The mind of the German Shepherd needs to be stimulated with directed play, organized activities, and challenging training. If that is absent, he can revert to simple prey drive, chasing whatever will run and getting himself into trouble in an urban setting.

The German Shepherd is a strong, intelligent, and active dog that needs the companionship of people and needs leadership to develop his potential. He is smart enough to do it all, but needs the right context in which to focus his great abilities.

BE PREPARED! The German Shepherd and Prey

You have finally found the perfect spot in the wilderness to walk him off lead, and you both love it. He never goes out of sight, staying close to protect you, and everything is delightful. Then, a rabbit is flushed from the bushes and away he goes, out of sight and out of control. Yelling does not stop him, and he uncharacteristically does not respond to you at all.

Welcome to the conflict between instinct and training. Training will ultimately win if repeated enough, but instinct can cause a terrible crisis in the meantime. Just rest assured, he is not lost. He has a better sense of direction than you do, and soon he will discover that he can't find the illusive rabbit and will come back.

The danger is in trying this exercise where he can move in a few seconds from an open space into a residential area, up to a barbed-wire fence or around other domestic animals. You have to think beyond the immediate pleasure of the walk to the potential dangers to your dog. Sometimes it is not easy. Keep on training....

Chapter Three

How to Choose a German Shepherd

Once you have made the decision to get a German Shepherd, you want to find a good one. As is true of all breeds, not all German Shepherds are good representatives of the breed or of the canine species in total. The goal is to find one that is compatible with your lifestyle, your neighborhood, and the task in which you want him involved.

There are those in our world who have bred the German Shepherd to be mean and to be an attack dog. A good German Shepherd is not mean. Although schutzhund trials and police work require a "hard" dog, that dog is trained to bite and hold as a game using its play drive. Although his job is to bite, he should never do so because he is vicious or mean.

The statement is often made that a German Shepherd without breed type is not worthy of being called a German Shepherd, but a German Shepherd without proper temperament is not worthy of being called a dog. It is for this reason that proper temperament in the German Shepherd is at the top of the standard's listing of attributes of the breed. The German Shepherd should be fearless, but not overly aggressive. Although he is not friendly with everyone, like a Golden Retriever or some small dog breeds, he should not be overtly unfriendly. The standard refers to the German Shepherd as "aloof," simply meaning that he is self-confident without the need for approval from everyone he meets. Most dogs who bite are reacting to a fearful situation. The German Shepherd should not be fearful, but don't expect him to jump up and kiss you either, until you are the owner and master.

When selecting a puppy, look for the one who is outgoing, happy, and confident. The shy puppy is often a fearful one. Socialization can help to bring him into the world of other dogs and people, but it may signal an improper temperament. Also be sure to evaluate the sire and dam of the litter. The puppy is a genetic product of the parents and will have characteristics similar to them. If the parents are shy and antisocial, there is a good chance the puppy will be also when he grows up.

You will want to be cautious of the source of the dog you choose and the skill of his breeder and the breeding decisions and practices.

German Shepherd Sources

There are many sources from which you may choose your new dog, but not all are equal. The sign on the street corner or in the newspaper may say, "German Shepherd Puppies—Championship Lines—Import Lines—Father over 125 lb." There are several warning signs here. Championship lines may mean that seven generations back there is a dog with a "Champion" in front of his name, but do we really know that the parents are even registered or are able to be registered? "Championship lines" does not tell you anything about the dog himself or how the breeding decision was made and what kind of health history was constructed before making that breeding decision.

Some breeders have bred for big German Shepherds, but the German Shepherd is not really a big dog. He is supposed to be a medium-sized dog, with the females between 22 and 24 inches tall (56–60 cm) at the shoulder and the males between 24 and 26 inches (60–66 cm). Although variations in height do occur and are not a major fault, to breed for an extreme can and has created some structural problems.

Also, the fact that the dog has a German-sounding name does not mean he was bred in Germany, nor does it mean he will be more healthy and sound. Although a good pedigree is a good thing, it does not imply that the breeding decision was a good one. The breeder should be familiar with the traits and weaknesses inherent in each line, both the dogs and the bitches, and have studied those lines to determine if they are breeding into a problem or away from one.

FYI: The GSD Club of America

Every breeder who belongs to the German Shepherd Dog Club of America is invited to sign the Breeders Code of Ethics. It is required for those who serve on the board of directors. The code specifies a pledge to

- maintain the highest standards of health and care;
- commit to the highest standards in breeding;
- exercise integrity in sales and placement;
- use a sales contract and guarantee;
- and other provisions.

The details of this code can be found on the GSDCA website.

Although not every ethical breeder signs this code and not all who sign it necessarily practice it, it is a good guide to follow in evaluating the breeder with whom you are going to do business.

Asking for references is not inappropriate and can be a valuable resource in finding the right breeder for you.

Beware of the breeder who, when asked what health problems exist in the breeder's lines, assures you that there are no health issues. Dogs, like humans, are the product of their genetic makeup, and one thing is certain: Our dogs, and we the owners, will get sick and ultimately die of something. Being aware of our family history and of those issues in our genetic makeup can, to some degree, be predictive of our future. So when you ask what health issues are in the line, you should expect an answer that honestly describes what those issues are and how the breeding is a move away from those issues.

Deciding on the Task and Job

One way to select a puppy is to start with you, the owner. Decide what interests you have in a dog. What would you like to do with the dog? What will be his job, and what activities will you want him to enjoy with you? Once you have decided this, you can research the clubs and dog sports that accompany those activities. Whether it is search and rescue, obedience, schutzhund, agility, hiking, or any number of other activities, there is probably a group of people near you who do these things together.

If you want your dog to learn personal protection, then a schutzhund club would be a good resource. Obedience clubs are very popular and usually hold regular competitions that you can work toward and in which you can participate. The holy grail of dog activities is the conformation show in which your dog is seen on national television winning the Westminster Ken-

CHECKLIST

Are You Ready for a German Shepherd?

Are you ready for a German Shepherd? Don't answer "yes" until you have checked off each item on the list.

✔ I have a fenced yard that is large enough for exercise and with a fence high enough to provide safety.

I have the necessary things for my German Shepherd's care and safety:

✔ A leash and collar
✔ Food dish and water dish
✔ Food
✔ First aid kit
✔ I am prepared to exercise him daily.
✔ I have a training program lined up.

✔ I have a relationship with a good veterinarian.
✔ I am prepared for daily grooming.
✔ I have mapped out places to take him for socialization where there are people, other animals, and interesting changes in environment.
✔ I am ready to lead him into healthy habits and not be dominated by him.
✔ I will spend time with him every day, just playing and loving him.
✔ I believe in positive-reinforcement training and will never lose my temper with him.

nel Club Show or becoming the Grand Victor (the number one select dog) at the German Shepherd Club Nationals, held once each year by the national breed club, attracting dogs from all over the nation and around the world. These are all fun things that you can get involved in that give your dog the opportunity to have disciplined training that brings out his natural abilities.

Each activity has a group of people surrounding it who breed for the activity in which they are involved. Not all dogs are suited for everything. Your best chance of finding the right dog for you is in finding the people who breed for the purpose or job you desire for you and your dog.

Once you have decided on an activity or two, you may want to go to some of the club meetings and activities that are held for the dogs. This will give you a better background in your search for the right dog.

Finding a Breeder

Although the newspapers and local pet stores are resources for finding a dog, they may limit your options. In the case of the pet store, you may not have the information you need from the breeder unless the store has developed a communication with the breeder. And in the case of the newspaper, you may find a "backyard breeder" who, as well meaning as he may be, does not have the experience and the education to know how to make a quality breeding decision.

Just remember: The cost of the puppy is not the cost of the dog. Finding the cheapest puppy may not be economically wise if you end up with a lot of health problems or surgeries. All breeding programs are not equal, and the resulting puppies, as cute as they may be, are only as good as the genetics involved.

The Internet is another way to find available puppies, but just like any other means of communication, you are being told what the seller wants you to hear. Before you buy, you need to become knowledgeable enough to be able to ask the right questions and screen the negotiations to the essential ingredients.

Parent-club websites and regional club websites will usually include a list of breeders. This does not guarantee that the breeder is knowledgeable, but it does mean the person is probably involved with the breed and the other people who also are.

Screening for Health

There are a number of screening tools available to breeders today that were not available 40 years ago. The Orthopedic Foundation for Animals (OFA) offers several tests to dog breeders and owners. The OFA is the primary agency for the certification of hips and elbows in dogs. Historically, the German Shepherd has been among those breeds showing the highest incidence of hip dysplasia, typically listed in the top three. But since the advent of the OFA certification, the German Shepherd has dropped to number 39 in

OFA ranking, a significant reduction that removes this particular disease as the primary concern in the breed.

This has been achieved because high-quality breeders have simply refused to breed sires or dams who are not certified or do not have at least three of the past five generations on both sides of the pedigree who are certified. The German "A" stamp is similar to the OFA certification and has also been used as a breeding tool by reputable import breeders to reduce dysplasia. There are other health issues that a breeder needs to be aware of, and it is okay to ask if they use the German "A" stamp and if not, ask why not. American-bred and import lines have different issues. Heart problems and hemophilia are not big issues in the American-bred lines but are in some import lines. Degenerative myelopathy (DM) and bloat/torsion are of concern in the American lines and are not as prevalent in import lines. So a breeder

Breed Needs

Leaving the Litter

The breed club, most veterinarians, and most breeders recommend that a puppy not leave his mother or the pack until he is at least eight weeks old. There are essential stages of adjustment and socialization that happen in these early days, and he needs the comfort of his own kind. Some breeders will want to watch him a few more weeks to make sure he is adjusting well and is ready for his big transfer.

Occasionally a breeder is watching the puppies to see which ones will go to show homes, and this will take a little more time. Be patient. Leaving the litter too soon can be difficult for your little guy!

may not test for all possible problems unless those problems have some probability of being in their breeding.

What is important is that the breeder is aware of the issues and is breeding away from them by making informed decisions with a health history on both the sire and the dam. At the very least, because of the history of hip dysplasia, the breeder should be using either the German "A" stamp certification or the OFA certification.

One note: OFA does not certify hips until the dog is two years old, so any advertisement that says "OFA puppies" might warrant caution. You are looking for OFA-certified parents, not OFA-certified puppies.

The Secondhand German Shepherd

The GSDCA and its regional clubs have an extensive system of German Shepherd rescue resources. Other registries and performance clubs also pay attention to those dogs from this breed that are previously owned. And of course, city and county animal shelters have dogs of all breeds turned in to them from time to time. The problem is, not everything that is called a German Shepherd is a German Shepherd. "Erect ears does not a German Shepherd make." Interestingly, a dog with one-fourth or less of German Shepherd blood may still have some color or distinguishing features that seem to invite its being labeled as a German Shepherd.

If you think that a rescue Shepherd is what you want, then an Internet search for rescue organizations might be a good resource, or you can simply

FYI: Shelters and Rescue Groups

To find a shelter or rescue group near you, check out these helpful resources:

The American German Shepherd Rescue Association is a nationwide network of German Shepherd breeders.

Pet Finders matches your zip code to available animals of which they are aware.

Your regional German Shepherd Dog Club will be involved with rescue.

Check with your local city or county shelter. Occasionally they will have a German Shepherd.

Caution: Not everything that is called a German Shepherd is a German Shepherd. It is common to have anything with erect ears or a black saddle called a German Shepherd. Every dog, regardless of his breeding, needs a loving home, but if you are looking for a German Shepherd, be careful.

Older rescue dogs are a particularly sad situation. These dogs have given their whole life in love to someone who cannot or will not care for them any longer. They can bond strongly with those who give them a home for their remaining years, and there is a special place in heaven for those who do! Old dogs rule!

visit the GSDCA website and find a rescue person near you. This network of rescue people is committed to rescuing any purebred German Shepherd, whether a member animal or not. What's important to them is the dog, not where he came from.

Usually the rescue German Shepherd will be an adult, sometimes, unfortunately, an older dog that no one wants anymore. One of the usual and expected questions is, Can this dog learn to love another person, and will he ever be attached to me? The answer is simple: Yes! Dogs, unlike us people, tend to live in the moment and do not harbor grudges or carry rejection for long. He will willingly respond to a safe place to sleep, sufficient food to eat, and a warm and gentle hand to love him.

CAUTION

If the sire and dam of the litter are not present, it is more difficult to evaluate the litter. The genetics of the puppy determine his size, health, temperament, and various characteristics.

Be careful which puppy you choose, also. Tell the breeder about your lifestyle and time constraints, and they will be able to help guide you toward the right puppy. The breeder has watched them from birth, whereas you get to see them for only a short while, so the breeder might be able to help you make a better decision than just pointing at the cutest one.

Those who rescue have a special place in heaven. Those who adopt the rescued German Shepherd have that same special place.

Your local animal shelter and your regional GSDCA will have contact information for rescue organizations in your area. A good rescue organization will usually screen the temperament of the dog and try to match the dog to the family to which he goes. Often great dogs are given to rescue organizations for reasons having to do with the owners, not the dog. And yet, there are dogs that are given to rescue because the owners cannot deal with behavior or health problems. Be careful to screen any potential adoptive dog for temperament or health issues. Rescue organizations can be a great place to find a great dog or a place where problem dogs are passed on to someone else. Caution is important. Ask about your potential pet's history and reason for his being placed in rescue.

The Hobby Breeder

Of all the resources for finding your new puppy or dog, one of the best is the local hobby breeder. This is a person who is a fanatic about the breed and is involved in a regional club and in the sport they enjoy. Even if you are looking only for a family pet to accompany the family around the block and on camping trips and to be there in the home to love and protect, the hobby breeder can be your best resource.

This breeder likely knows the issues of the breed, and if they do not have available puppies, they probably know who does. They probably will also have raised their puppies in their home, will be familiar with the personalities, and will be able to match you with the right puppy. There are even some breeders who will not allow the buyer to pick the puppy but will make the choice themselves. As offensive as that may sound to some, it is not always a bad idea.

You will probably find that the knowledgeable hobby breeder charges more than the breeder with no club network and active participation in a sport or activity with their dogs. That is simply because there are costs involved in doing it right. They involve the veterinary care of the sire and dam, as well as the puppies, the health checks and certifications, the proper shots and nutrition, and, in general, a greater attention to detail and the health of the breeding. And yet, the knowledgeable hobby breeder seldom makes any profit from their breeding. Most of these breeders are in it for the love of the breed and do not expect to make a profit.

Helpful Hints

A good place to find reputable hobby breeders:

- Look at the German Shepherd Dog Club of America website at *www.GSDCA.org* and find the regional breed club in your area.
- Contact the regional club and ask for a reference to a good breeder.
- Find an all-breed club or obedience club in your area and ask them for the name of a good breeder of German Shepherds in your area.
- Call a few veterinary clinics and ask which veterinarian specializes in German Shepherds, and then call them and ask for a referral.
- Visit dog shows in your area and talk to exhibitors (when they are not in the ring or preparing their dog to go in—they cannot talk when preparing to show).

BE PREPARED! Ten Questions the Breeder Will Ask You

1. Why do you want a German Shepherd, and what will you be doing with him?
2. Do you have any experience with a German Shepherd, or have you had one in the past?
3. Do you have the necessary time, energy, and money to care for the needs of your new dog?
4. Do you have a fenced yard and a place to regularly exercise your German Shepherd?
5. Do you have children in the home and other pets? If you have other dogs, what sex are they? Are you willing to choose an opposite-sexed German Shepherd for compatibility?
6. How many hours a day are you home? Are there others in the home who will spend time with your German Shepherd?
7. Can you provide the name of your veterinarian and at least three references who can speak to your ability to care for your pets?
8. Will you be able to bring all members of the family to visit the breeder's kennel before the puppy goes home with you?
9. Will your German Shepherd accompany you on vacations, and if not, how will he be cared for?
10. Will you promise to return the German Shepherd to the breeder if at any time you are no longer able to care for him?

Although some of these items may seem intrusive, please understand that most breeders are not selling a product; they are placing a living being under your care. They look at it as an adoption process more than as the sale of a commodity.

You will probably find that the hobby breeder has a waiting list for his dogs, but not all puppies in a litter are going to be show dogs, so there may be some in each litter that are available to pet homes.

Red Flags

Hobby breeders especially are going to be very particular when choosing a home for their puppy. That's right! This is not a matter of your deciding to buy a puppy. Many breeders will not allow you to have their puppy without first checking you out. Although there are those who will be offended by that practice, it is born out of an ethic that sees a lifetime responsibility for what the breeder brings into the world. They will want certain guarantees from you, including a commitment to return the dog at any point that you cannot keep him. Most breeders do not want to ever find their stock in a shelter.

So, it is best not to start by asking what the price will be. Those who are interested only in a cheap price will raise flags for the breeder. You will want

BE PREPARED! Ten Questions to Ask the Breeder

1. How old are the puppies, and what sexes are in the litter?
2. Are the parents of the litter registered with a recognized kennel club, such as the AKC?
3. Is the litter registered, and will the puppy come with an individual registration form?
4. Have the puppies been examined by a veterinarian and had their first vaccinations? What vaccinations have the puppies received?
5. Have the puppies been treated for any internal and external parasites?
6. Have the parents been OFA certified for hips and elbows, and is there a five-generation record of OFA certifications?
7. What are the health problems in the pedigree? Has there been any testing or planning to see that they are eliminated or limited in this litter?
8. What food are the puppies on and how often are they fed?
9. Will you be able to see the parents of the litter or pictures of the sire if he is not on-site?
10. Will the breeder take the puppy back if at some point you are unexpectedly unable to care for him?

to ask about health histories, certifications for the parents, and so forth. This shows that you are knowledgeable and are interested in the quality of the breeding.

Look at the condition of the home and kennel. It may be a clue as to how careful this breeder is with the rest of their program. This check is not a matter of perfect housekeeping but of general order and sanitation.

Ask about the breeder's involvement with an organized dog sport, such as hunting, showing, or obedience.

Ask what organizations they belong to that are dog related.

Ask if they have signed the GSDCA Breeders Code of Ethics. This does not guarantee that they follow it, but it may provide some indication about their ethics in breeding.

Ask questions and expect questions in return. Ultimately, the relationship with your breeder should become one that is ongoing throughout the life of the dog.

Choosing the Perfect Puppy

Once you have found the right breeder, it is time to select the right puppy. There are few things more exhilarating than the prospects of finding the right one. In some cases, the breeder will assess you and then decide which puppy they feel is the best fit for you and your family. This is not usual, but it is not

uncommon, and depending on how good they are at assessing people, it may work very well.

Do not expect them to bring out the entire litter, however. If you are not a show person looking for that rare show prospect, then the breeder will keep the show prospects back and not show them. These dogs are not for sale unless you are going to show them. However, this may be a good time to ask the breeder about showing and a good time to make that commitment to get involved. Be careful, however, for making a commitment to show your new puppy will alter your schedule and cost you money, all of which will be well spent. It is a great sport with which to get involved.

When looking over the puppies, look for the one who is alert, attentive, and even mischievous. There are also some simple tests you might want to do. One is to place a treat on the floor or ground and then place a can over it. Especially with this breed you would expect the puppy to make an assumption that it is under there because he

saw it and knows you hid it. This power of deduction indicates a level of intelligence you would expect from the German Shepherd. You can also do the sleight-of-hand trick in which you place the treat between your thumb and first finger and then cover it with the other hand, dropping the treat into the hand while pretending to grab it with the covering hand. Again, when you reveal that the treat is no longer in the hand it appeared to be in, we would like to see the puppy go to the other hand, assuming that the treat is there somewhere.

If the breeder has done trust exercises with the puppy, you should be able to hold him while turning him on his back. A dog that will not permit this does not want to lose control, whereas one that too easily allows this may not be as strong as you might want. An extreme reaction one way or the other will give some indication of how the puppy views his world.

The Papers

Typically a puppy will come with a written contract and guarantee. He will also come with a registration certificate to the registry under which he was bred. Of course, he is not a machine put together on an assembly line. He is

PERSONALITY POINTERS
Puppy Aptitude Test

Test Purpose	How to Test
Social Attraction Sociability and interest in people	Coax the puppy to come to you.
Following Interest in people and dependence/independence	Get his attention and then walk away.
Restraint Dominant versus submissive	Pick the puppy up and roll him on his back in your arms.
Social Dominance Willingness to interact with people	Stroke the puppy on the back while he is standing.
Intelligence Ability to reason	Hide a morsel of food under a can or in another hand.
Retrieving Instinctive response to retrieve	Throw a ball, toy, or wad of paper out from the puppy.
Sound Sensitivity Sensitivity to loud or unfamiliar sounds	Make a sharp noise, clap, or drop keys on a hard surface a few feet from him.
Touching Sensitivity Measures sensitivity to being handled	Gently press the webbing between his toes, and feel his pads.
Sight Sensitivity Measures visual sensitivity to moving objects	Tie a string to a towel and then wave it near him.

Note: These tests are highly subjective. They are used in guide dog selection programs but are not always done correctly by novice puppy buyers. So try them, but do not be too aggressive in their administration, and use them only to see the differences between each puppy.

What to Look For	Results
Does he come eagerly, eventually, or not at all. Does he run away or cower?	The GSD is aloof, so he may not respond quickly to strangers, but does he come and show confidence?
Does he follow eagerly, hesitate or not come at all, or run the other way?	The GSD is aloof, but the more social puppy will eventually follow.
Does he protest and struggle to regain control, immediately give up, or go limp and urinate?	He should struggle somewhat at first. Any lack of struggle may indicate lack of confidence.
Does he protest, run away, lick the tester, or roll over immediately?	If he enjoys the petting, this is ideal. Rolling over or running away may show fear of people.
If he looks for the missing food, he has reasoned that it was there and still is. If he walks away, he has not made that logical conclusion.	The curious and persistent puppy has made a reasoned conclusion.
Does the puppy chase it, pick it up, and try to bring it back?	Prey drive will make him go after the object. This might be a good dog for sporting activities.
Does he bark, investigate, or shy away?	Interest without fear is best, but being protective is appropriate also in the adult. Puppies should not exhibit aggressiveness. Running is not good.
How long does it take him to protest?	He should not be scared, but should be annoyed after a few seconds.
Does he chase and play with the towel, just look at it, or run away?	The one who looks interested and isn't threatened or aggressive is the best choice.

Chapter Four

Caring for a German Shepherd Puppy

Before you bring your puppy home, it is good to prepare for the event. One of the first things to do is to puppy-proof your home. Do a walk-through with a pad and pencil and write down anything you may need to rearrange or change. There will be things that are down at puppy level and the puppy will not know they are not his. Here is your chance to see through the eyes of the dog, which will become a lifelong skill as you live with your new best friend.

If it smells good, he will find it. So learn to put people food and dog food in a secure place. Be sure your floors and low shelves are free of valuable knickknacks or other small objects that could be dangerous to the puppy. Be aware of household chemicals and keep them tightly sealed and out of reach.

Be aware of the foods that are good for humans but poisonous for dogs. Chocolate, grapes, raisins, alcohol, and others can be poisonous to your pet and should be out of his reach. Folding gates or folding exercise pens can help to create barriers to keep the puppy out of areas that you prefer he not go.

There are also plants that are poisonous, such as poinsettias and others in that family of plants. Become familiar with them and protect your puppy. He will not know what is good for him or bad for him. His primary sense of touch is with his mouth, so he will put everything you leave down in his mouth.

Preparing for a Puppy

There are some things your puppy will need right from the start. He will need a place to sleep and bedding on which to sleep. The German Shepherd is a den animal and likes a place of his own that is safe and enclosed. A dog crate is a good way to give him that den, and he will learn to love it in short order.

A crate is also a great way to housetrain your puppy. If he sleeps in his crate at night, then take him outside first thing in the morning and praise him when he goes potty outside. Then it is your responsibility to watch him during the day. When he has a nap, put him outside immediately when he wakes up and praise him again when he goes. Also watch when he is

wandering about with his nose down, sniffing. This can be a sign he is looking for a spot to go potty.

If you do not recognize that he needs to go, it is your fault, not his. He does not yet know where or when nature calls. He will go when he needs to, wherever he is. It is your responsibility to show him where, when he signals the time. Housetraining is usually quite easy for the German Shepherd, and is accomplished within a day or two. It happens faster when you are attentive and on top of it.

The puppy will also need fresh water available at all times of the day and night. He does not perspire as we do, cooling himself through his mouth and by his breathing and panting patterns. So having fresh water is more than getting a drink; it is also a means of maintaining body temperature.

CAUTION

If the puppy has access to the garage, be sure there is no antifreeze stored anywhere. It has a sweet taste and for some reason is attractive to dogs, but a small amount, even licked off his paws, can kill him in a matter of minutes.

Food is the other thing that needs to be decided upon before bringing your puppy home. Your breeder can tell you what the puppy is eating before you bring him home, and it might be good to continue that for a while before making a change. Too many changes at once may be upsetting.

There are a lot of good puppy foods and dog foods available these days. The most expensive may not be the best, but then again it might indicate the quality of the ingredients. Ask your breeder, your veterinarian, or the expert at the pet store. Although an expensive food is not necessary, the cheapest is probably not a good choice. Using a premium dog food may pay dividends in the long run.

Puppy foods are higher in protein than adult dog foods and can be safely used for the first six months in most breeds. Many German Shepherd breeders believe that a puppy should be switched to adult food sooner than six months because it may contribute to some structural problems. Panosteoitis is one of the issues of inflammation in the large bones of the growing puppy that many breeders and veterinarians link to the feeding of too much protein. Check with your veterinarian about when he recommends switching to adult food.

Puppy Supplies

Crate or Kennel

A good time to go shopping is before you bring the puppy home. Although he may enjoy nestling into a pile of old blankets, you might want to be prepared so he has his own bedding. A good crate pad is a lasting item he will learn to love. You will also want a crate for his comfort and safety. He will love his "den" in no time and will

retreat to it when he wants to be alone and sleep. There are several types. Folding wire crates are convenient to move and to travel with but are not accepted on airlines. Hard-shell plastic crates are accepted by airlines but are more difficult to carry around. Your lifestyle and the expected job for your German Shepherd will dictate what kind you get. There are also some newer fabric crates that seem convenient and might work for a small, quiet breed. They may not be a lasting investment for a German Shepherd, though.

The crate or kennel will also become a welcome tool when the repair man comes to fix the sink or the delivery man brings in a package. Although you can expect the dog to respond to your training, he is territorial and will want to protect you and the house. He should, however, be social with your friends and those who are invited into the house. Even so, when friends come over for dinner, the crate might be a good place for your dog to go away from the table at dinnertime. Your training will include the puppy, and later the dog, being with people and your guests, but not all guests enjoy the presence of a dog, so the crate can be useful in protecting him from people who are less than friendly to his presence.

Food and Water Containers

A good food dish and water bowl are also essential. Although many materials and styles are available, consider that a stainless-steel dish may outlast several plastic ones. Be sure to think past the puppy stage. Buying puppy sized items may be cute, but your dog will be small for only a few weeks. He will be adult sized in body sooner than you might think or even want.

It is not a bad idea to provide a safe, dry container for the dog kibble, either. A sack of food, stored at dog level, might be more than you want to leave to chance.

Leash, Collar, and ID

There are literally hundreds of options when it comes to this category. Collars come in plastic, nylon, woven fabric, and a variety of chain styles. Similarly there are a plethora of leads. In making your choice, consider yourself as well as your dog. You have chosen a powerful, strong dog, and you can easily damage a hand or finger with the wrong equipment.

For training, you will want a simple "choke collar." This type of collar has a bad reputation because of its misuse by those who rely on high levels of emotion and struggle against their dog to gain compliance. We'll cover training in another section, but remember: We do not gain compliance by pain or by force. Your dog will want to learn and obey. The collar is simply a means of exercising the control you will gain by the training. He will learn that a slight tug or snap of the leash and collar means something and will learn to respond without heavy force and to move with the handler.

Breed Needs

Dog seat belts are available now, but your German Shepherd may not benefit as much as a smaller dog. His size may make his sitting in a car seat impractical. Having a car that can accommodate his crate is ideal. He will love to ride in his crate so he can watch outside and also nap as he needs to. Crates can also accommodate a small stainless-steel bucket, clipped to the side, for water.

You will also want a collar to which you can attach some identification when you are out with the dog running in the field. This is far less important with the German Shepherd than with most other breeds. The reason is that although the German Shepherd may run into the field to explore, he is primarily a herding dog. He will seldom go beyond having you in sight. That is not to say that a rabbit will not entice him to a grand chase over a hill, but he should not be far away. Some breeds will run until they cannot find their way back. That is not typical of the German Shepherd.

Leads come in various sizes, shapes, and materials also. A good leather lead, when broken in, is probably the most comfortable in the hand and flexible for use in training.

Never leave a collar on your dog in his crate or in his yard. There are far too many stories of dogs that have choked to death by getting hung up on a fence or some other obstacle.

Oh yes, and while we are here, let's talk a little bit about fencing. A good fence is essential. If you live in a rural area with open spaces and no close neighbors, you need a fence to protect your dog from the wildlife that is natural to those areas. If you live in the city with a small yard and close neighbors, you will need a fence to protect your dog from the wildlife that is natural to those areas (children, people, and other dogs). If you live anywhere, you need a fence to protect both the dog and the neighborhood. Here's a good rule of thumb with the German Shepherd: No fence, no dog.

Helpful Hints

Although a good-quality leather lead may be more expensive, it may also be easier on your hands. As your puppy grows up, he will become stronger, and many leads will be hard on your hands. Leather will become softer and better with use and age and usually outlasts most other materials.

Although board fences may be more expensive, they also provide privacy. This might be attractive to the neighborhood and our people senses, but might be frustrating to the German Shepherd. A woven wire fence will provide for sight but may also tempt that rare escape artist to climb. You will have to choose based on your community and your desires, but make sure it is a high fence. A 6 foot fence (1.8 m) should be adequate for most German Shepherds.

Toys and Snacks

Some veterinarians recommend against chew sticks, chew bones, or anything that, when rehydrated, swells up. The fact that it is available in the pet store does not mean it is a good idea. Some foreign-produced chew snacks have been found to be preserved with formaldehyde or other harmful products. Be careful what you give your dog for a toy or a snack. It is best to ask your veterinarian. They have experienced many tragedies from pets being injured or killed by a toy or snack given with good intentions. There are many commercial snacks available, and he will probably like some and ignore others. Trying several dog treats may help you decide. Carrots are usually a favored treat by dogs and of course the microwaved hot dog slice is also a standard.

The German Shepherd will love to play ball, fetch, and tug. Toys that are not small enough to be swallowed and that can be used for these activities will be a welcome treat. The longstanding favorites are the tennis ball and the braided tug toy. Smaller balls that can be swallowed or become lodged in the throat are to be avoided. He will also absolutely adore stuffed toys. Some stuffed toys have filling that, if ingested, becomes impacted in the intestines. Check with your veterinarian for guidance and be sure that his stuffed toys are safe for dogs. These can be found everywhere, including garage sales and thrift stores, with the understanding that with the German Shepherd

the toy's life span is limited. Make sure the toys are clean and that the eyes are removed. If you don't remove them, your dog will in short order. If he swallows them, he might be fine, but then again you don't want to chance an expensive surgery to remove them. A good rule of thumb is that when the stuffing is exposed, the toy is dead and should be buried in the trashcan. You might also want to avoid those toys stuffed with Styrofoam beads. Cleanup may be impossible with these.

Another good piece of equipment is a toy box. He will love to go shopping in his toy box for the toy of his choice at the moment. Some dogs can also be easily trained to put their toys in the box—well, sometimes.

Stain- and Odor-Removing Spray

Accidents will happen. They will happen in the course of housetraining, when your dog is upset and has diarrhea, and when he is sick and throws up. Like people, he will have physical upsets from time to time. It is best to prepare for it. There are a variety of products on the market with varying degrees of effectiveness and some commercial products that are more expensive and also do a better job. The most effective may not tell you that their active ingredients are hydrogen peroxide *(Note: This can "bleach" fabric)*, washing soda, and dish soap. Do not add bleach to this mixture or you will cause a dangerous chemical reaction and everything it touches will turn white. Be sure to rinse thoroughly. If in doubt, try some of the new commercial products available at the supermarket or your pet supply store. Many are quite good.

Grooming Supplies

The German Shepherd is called the "wash-and-wear dog"—that is, grooming and bathing are easier than for most other breeds. He will need regular brushing to remove dead hair and an occasional bath, but since he does not have sweat glands like people, he does not smell as bad or as quickly as people. You will know when it is time to give him a bath.

A good soft-bristle brush is adequate. Some of the pin brushes remove dead hair better, but can also irritate the skin and hurt your dog. Making grooming a positive experience is always a worthy objective. A "rake" grooming tool serves to supplement the soft-bristle brush, getting down into the undercoat and removing the more stubborn dead hair. This is important in hotter, more humid climates where hot spots can become an issue on his skin.

Clipping Nails

Clipping your German Shepherd's nails can be quite a chore. The best way is to start him young and do it regularly. One tool that some learn to like is the Dremel Tool. Simply hold the paw, separating the toes as you move along and grind the nail tip off.

Nail clippers are also a useful item. Nails should be trimmed every week or so, depending on the area where you live and the surface on which your dog lives. Some dogs do not have fast-growing nails and can wear them down walking, running, and digging. Yes, he is a dog and he will dig. Can you break him from this? You can try, but it is easier to give him a place where he can dig and let him! He is not a varmint dog, so he will not be as inclined to dig as some breeds, but he is a dog with nails for digging.

To clip the nails, you might want to train him to climb onto a grooming table, couch, or other place where you can easily reach him and he can lie down. Clipping a little off the tip regularly is better than trying to catch up to not trimming more regularly. Also, be careful not to cut into the quick of the nail. Dog nails bleed easily, and sometimes it seems the bleeding will never stop. It is better to avoid this and to have some septic powder on hand in case you make a mistake. If you lift the foot so you can see the backside of the nail, you will see where the quick stops and the nail continues. Cutting below that dividing line will keep the nail from bleeding.

Washing the Dog

A gentle dog shampoo is better than dish soap or other soap not designed for sensitive skin. There are some good products available, and some are made for dogs in areas where fleas and ticks prevail. Some German Shepherds are allergy prone, and it would be good to find a shampoo specifically designed for this if your dog has coat allergies. It is essential to remove all the shampoo residue. As the old saying goes, wash once, rinse twice. This will eliminate most reactions to the chemicals in the shampoo. Also be sure to dry him carefully in cold temperatures or in humid climates. A wet dog can be a joy to watch as he enjoys being wet, but a wet coat also will retain body heat in

hot climates and can be dangerous in cold temperatures. To dry him, use a dryer without heat, a vacuum with a reverse blowing function, or a dog dryer. Blow until he looks dry, and then feel the coat. He will look dry before he is. Keep blowing until the undercoat is dry and he feels dry.

Brushing His Teeth

It is also a good idea to get him used to having his teeth brushed. There are some good doggie toothbrushes available, or a human one is acceptable. Doggie tooth paste is also available in various flavors from liver to mint. He will tell you which he prefers. Remember, dogs do not spit, so human tooth-paste is not recommended because some ingredients can be toxic for dogs, particularly some noncaloric sweeteners found in human toothpastes, and other products.

The First Night—Creating Safety

If you have children, remember back to the day the baby came home. What a wonderful day that was—except that it was followed by nighttime. Think about what is going on for the puppy when he comes home to your house. He has been surrounded by his mother, his breeder, and his littermates for his entire life. Yes, to us it is but a brief time, but to him, it is eternity. He is taken from the routine he has learned and the environment he loves and is familiar with and dropped into total chaos.

He will not know what is expected of him or what to do. All he will know is when he is hungry and scared. It is your job to allow him to learn the new surroundings and adapt to the new routine. You might want to temporarily make a place for his crate next to your bed, where you can talk to him in the night and hold him if necessary. Yes, this is much like bringing the new baby home. Your routine, like your new puppy's, will never be the same.

Trying to enforce rules of behavior or territory probably should wait until the puppy has settled in. The puppy will need to know where to sleep, where to eat, where his bathroom is, and who these people are around him. Although family and friends will want to come and visit your new puppy, it can also add to the confusion for him at first. Waiting a day or two for visitors is not a bad idea.

Some people like to start potty training with a newspaper and then move the paper toward the door and finally outside. Others provide access to the outside and start by watching and helping the little fellow make the decision from the start. The latter method shortens the process, but you will have to be with the puppy all the time to enable his getting outside when he needs to go.

You might experience a lot of whining and fussing the first few nights. This is to be expected and is not a matter for discipline. It is a need for security and comfort, so do what you can to provide support, and a warm stuffed toy or two, and wait it out. He will adapt.

Breed Needs

Most contracts from a breeder, shelter, or rescue group will require a visit to your veterinarian within the first day or two. You will want to do it as soon as possible to assure that the puppy is in good health. Should you find some health problem, it is important to let the breeder know immediately for the safety of the rest of the litter and to protect your contract rights. (See page 43.)

Puppies are biological creatures, not mechanically assembled products, so they will have faults and problems just as we humans do. Contracts can guarantee health only for a limited period of time, so make sure to follow their provisions.

The First Day—Creating a Space

Your puppy's first day can be a delightful time of exploring the yard. If you bring him home in the daytime, rather than take him inside, assume he will need to go potty and take him into the yard, at least until he goes potty. Exploring his yard will be an exciting time for him and he will do so by instinct, smelling everything. Remember, his nose is his ticket to his world and is his primary sense, so give him time to sniff it out and understand his new environment. Make sure you do not have poisonous plants in the yard before he gets there.

This first day is also a good time to introduce him to his new toys and to let him select which are going to be his favorites. Unfortunately, the pink pullover sweater Aunt Ethel made him may not be his favorite.

SHOPPING LIST

New Puppy Supplies

You can make a copy of this list and take it to the pet supply store with you. This will help you not to forget something you may need for your German Shepherd puppy.

✔ Crate or kennel for housetraining, safety, and travel
✔ Soft bedding or a kennel pad for the crate or kennel
✔ Pet seat belt or strap for the kennel or crate
✔ Leash
✔ High-quality puppy food
✔ Metal or ceramic food and water dishes
✔ Soft, natural-bristle brush
✔ Nail trimmer or grinding tool

✔ Gentle dog shampoo
✔ Toothbrush and toothpaste for dogs
✔ Safe chew toys
✔ Stain and odor remover for house-training accidents

Optional:
✔ Dog bed
✔ Play toys
✔ Fetching dumbbell
✔ Tug toy
✔ Healthful treats or cookies
✔ Extra collar
✔ Extra leash
✔ Pet gates
✔ Outdoor doghouse
✔ Dog travel gear, for food, water, and toys

After you take him inside, be sure to take him back out every 15 to 20 minutes, because puppies potty frequently and it happens fast. Again, his failure to be trained from the start is not his fault and is not a matter for discipline. Housetraining is the owner's responsibility, not the puppy's. You have to learn to read the signs and put him out. Rubbing his nose in it, hitting him with a newspaper, and throwing him out the door is not a good method, unless you want to teach him to rub his own nose in it, hit himself with a newspaper, and then run out the door. Repetition and consistency is the best method. He will learn fast, and you will be surprised at how easily he catches on.

Be sure to clap and praise him when he does it right. The neighbors may think you're crazy, constantly clapping, and saying, "good poo poo!" But then, the neighbors probably think you are anyway for bringing another dog into the neighborhood. What your dog thinks is the most important.

Meeting the Family

People will want to come over and meet the new puppy and hold him. The big caution here is disease. Your puppy should have had at least his first shots and have some immunity from that and from his mother, but some people are less than careful, and your puppy's safety is your responsibility.

If your guests do not have pets, there is probably not a problem, but if they do, just touch base with them about their animals' immunization. Some people do not believe in immunizing their animals, and although you always want to honor their firmly held belief system, you also do not want to compromise the health of your new puppy.

A good rule of thumb is to give the puppy a few days with the immediate family before inviting guests to come and see him. This will give him time to bond with family members and to understand who is part of the human family (pack). He will catch on in no time and will be able to "read" the family members as his circle of acquaintances enlarges.

Although socialization is something you want to encourage, there are some cautions you might want to enforce. The first is the safety of the people playing with the puppy. Your puppy will have razor-sharp teeth and nails and in his enthusiasm can easily draw blood. In time you will teach your puppy not to jump up and bite your arms, but initially he will not know the difference between arms and toys. Be careful of little children who want to visit the puppy. It is okay, but they might come away with some scratches and marks. Make sure they are either ready for it or able to refrain from playing with the puppy.

The other caution is about picking up the puppy and carrying him around. Again, it is good for the puppy to be handled and socialized and to learn that people like to handle him, but you do not want to have him dropped either because the person holding him is too young or the puppy is too wiggly to make this exercise work safely. So, let people come and play and hold, but take care for the safety of the puppy and the guests. Either may try to play too hard at first.

Meeting Other Pets

If you have other pets in the home, your new German Shepherd should meet them as soon as is practical. Just make sure they do not overwhelm him at first and that you are clearly the leader of the pack in the introduction. The German Shepherd puppy will want to explore the other pets and play with them, but will usually resist being dominated by them. If the other dogs in the pack are breeds that are not as dominant, your German Shepherd will probably end up being the alpha pet in the pack. You will not have to determine those roles; the pack will just work them out. You will have to monitor the process, however, for it can become violent if the existing alpha is strong. An intact young male may challenge that leadership if the older male leader weakens or is unsure of his leadership. You will have to monitor the process. Keeping the older dogs separate but present can be accomplished with X-pens or doggie gates until their familiarity with the puppy grows to inclusion in the pack. All packs have a leader, and the leader will fight to keep dominance of his pack. You do not want your new puppy to be a casualty of this process, so constant supervision is essential until pack roles and pack acceptance has been established.

Helpful Hints

Older pets already in the home are probably territorial too. They may resent this new creature in their space and the attention he gets. It is a good idea to remember this and to include the older pets in the process with lots of praise and attention also.

If a conflict develops between two alpha dogs, monitor it and help them work it out without injury. It is usually best not to combine two females or two males in the pack.

If there is aggression on the part of the older adults or fear on the part of the puppy, it will be important to keep them separate until you work that out with them. In some cases, two dogs will not be able to be in the same pack. Usually it is two dogs of the same sex, in which case the illusion of one big happy family may not be in your future. Most breeders and experienced "dog people" with multiple breeds accept this fact and accommodate multiple dogs in multiple packs, keeping them separated. Two females may get along for a lengthy time, until one of them comes into heat, and then they may fight to the death. It is important to be aware of pack rules and pack dominance needs, and to keep dogs of the same sex separate when they are without supervision.

Before you even select your puppy, do so with your other pets in mind. Some breeds can live together easily regardless of their sex, but two German Shepherd bitches or two male dogs do not typically work well together. There are, of course, exceptions, but that is a good rule to follow.

Occasionally, the resident pets will not like this new intruder. They have their pack order and do not want to share their space or family with him. This is not uncommon or a matter of great concern. Sometimes a gradual introduction and then separation for a time will make the introduction easier. Let them set their own pace, and in time they will redefine the pack and all will be well. Occasionally, two dogs simply will not and cannot adjust to each other. In those cases, having separate protected space is necessary. Be sure to pay special attention to the old dogs of the house and give them more attention, treats, and toys while this transition is taking place. They need to feel more important and to associate good things with the presence of the new puppy.

CAUTION

Keep resident pets separate from the new German Shepherd unless you are present and in control. Conflict can arise from pack position, owner attention, and same-sex pack roles. Occasionally that conflict can be serious and permanent. Easy does it!

Time to Adjust

If your puppy has not been raised in a crate, he may consider it a jail for a short time. But he will need some quiet time, even on his first day. He will sleep a lot as a puppy, and providing a place where he can feel safe to do so is important. So, make sure the crate is in a comfortable place and out of the main traffic of the rest of the family and pack and let him get acquainted with it. Putting some toys inside and leaving the door open might be a good

start, but ultimately you will need to close the gate and lock it. Be prepared for some reaction, but comfort him until he is comfortable or asleep before leaving him alone.

As soon as he awakes from his nap, put him outside. Just as we need to go when we get up in the morning, so will he. Make sure that he has regular crate time through the day for his safety and training and for your own sanity.

Finally, you will need to go to the store, or take your own nap, or do a chore, and the puppy will be inconvenient, so he will need to go into the crate. His first time or two alone in the crate may be traumatic and elicit whines, barks, and howls. It is okay to let him fuss about it, but he will also need to know that he cannot bargain with his behavior. You are the owner. You are the alpha of the pack. You will be loving and kind, but you will also always win. That is the rule of the pack. After he settles down for a few minutes, it is time to let him come out and play again. By doing this you are reinforcing your control over the process and timing and also teaching that good behavior works better than fussing.

Fun Facts

Dogs sleep approximately 14 hours a day, so he will usually sleep when you do and need an additional six hours of sleep during the day.

Dogs also dream while sleeping, as we do. Watch for rapid eye movement and body twitches as indicators of his dreaming. Some dogs will move their legs as they dream of running in their sleep. This is normal and should not be a concern.

The Older Dog

If you have chosen an older dog or a rescue dog rather than a puppy, much of the above will apply. You should expect that he is housetrained, but there is no guarantee, so keep an eye on him, help him find his place, and make sure he has access. Older dogs may need a little more time to adjust to new surroundings and new people. They will also come from a social structure that is different and need time to absorb the pack structures of your home. They will miss their former territory, people, and social structures and need time to decide how to fit into the new roles. They may be anxious, fearful, or aggressive for a time. Helping them understand and adjust is as important as raising a puppy is. They simply will not know what is expected or who these new people are. They will need assurance that they are part of the family and an honored part of things. The older dog can bond with new people as firmly as the puppy, but he will need tender loving care in the process. It is good to assume nothing and to start from the beginning with the older dog as you would with a puppy, giving him a place to sleep, a place to go potty, and his own toys. Leash training cannot be assumed, nor in fact any training. Just remember, training is an act of love and should be always rewarded with lots of love, praise, and a treat or two.

Chapter Five

Living with a German Shepherd

You've brought your puppy home, and gotten him settled into a basic routine, so now you can go back to life as usual, right? No way. Life will never be the same. Your lifestyle is going to change in ways similar to bringing home a baby. Your schedule will be affected, your patterns of activities will change, and even your thinking will be altered. You have expanded your world and family to include another living thing that is going to be one of the great joys of your life.

Housetraining

Housetraining starts the moment your German Shepherd steps into your house. Fortunately, housetraining for our breed is not difficult and usually does not take long. The key is for you, the new owner, to learn to watch for and read the signs that the puppy needs to go out. It will probably be more frequent than you would like at first, but staying on top of it will shorten the time it takes and will also reduce your frustration with any accidents that might occur. Just remember, if the puppy goes on the carpet, it is not because he is stupid or rebellious. It is because you did not read the need beforehand.

The signs will be subtle until you learn to read them. Your puppy will start wandering and sniffing, and he will need to go more frequently than you might think. Taking him to his "spot" should happen every 15 to 20 minutes at first, and immediately when he wakes up. Vigilance will shorten the training time and reduce the cleanup time. It is good to praise him every time he goes to his spot and uses it. Before long, he will make the connection and start going on his own. Remember, however, that he will need access to his spot.

As the puppy learns where to go and how the routine of getting you to open the door works, he will also be lengthening the time between that need to go out and leaving you more time to go about your other responsibilities. This does not last forever. Installing a doggie door is one way to relieve the need to get up and down often and to also give your dog a sense of control over his body and environment.

HOME BASICS
It's Okay to Crate

Once a German Shepherd is crate trained, he will not mind going into his "den" for some quiet time. There are times when it is good for the family and for him to be secured: holiday gatherings, visits from friends who are afraid, and other times when his presence is simply intrusive to the circumstances. Just remember that a puppy cannot hold his bladder for long, and that even an adult is not designed to remain enclosed for lengthy periods of time. An hour or two is not unreasonable or punitive, but he should not be left for long hours in a crate, particularly unsupervised. If you are going to work or somewhere for a long period of time, your dog is better off in the yard. Whether in the yard or in the crate, he should always have a supply of fresh, clean water.

Crate Training

Crate training is another one of those things that does not take long and does not go on forever. In short order your German Shepherd will love his crate and go in it on his own if the door is open for his naptime. It's also a great way to train him for his travel time. Having a crate you can use in the house and in the car is a great way to make him feel safe and secure in the car as well.

To train him to his crate, simply leave the door open and put a treat inside, allowing him to retrieve it. As he is comfortable getting the treat, close the

door for a short period and then open it when he is not struggling against it. In short order, he will not fear the crate and will understand that he will be let out. You want the crate to be a positive thing and not a means of punishment. It is his den and is a safe place to be.

Schedule Training

The first rule of schedule training is that your schedule will be disrupted and subjected to change until you train your German Shepherd to your schedule. He will adapt and live through it, although he might try his best to train you to his schedule for some period of time.

He will sleep up to 14 hours a day and may decide that he likes sleeping in the day better than at night. Your employer, however, might like you to sleep at night and stay awake on the job. So, someone has to determine what the family's schedule will be. It might be best if you take that responsibility and do the training.

The German Shepherd does like a routine and to have things orderly, so he will adapt to your schedule if you will teach what that is and enforce it. One place to start is in sleep training. For the first few nights it might seem that this will never work, but rest assured, he will get the idea and will settle into the routine of sleeping nights. One of the easiest ways is to use the crate to reinforce when sleep should happen.

In early puppyhood, he will need to go out more often to potty, but even that needs to be trained so that he is retaining for longer periods of time at night and is free to go potty at will during the day. Having him sleep in his crate at night not only gives you some rest but also trains him to certain sleep hours and a potty routine.

Most biological creatures will slip into certain body routines in eating, sleeping, eliminating, and so forth. But if we are not regular in our routine, nature can be confused and the body will react with irregular patterns that are disruptive. Your German Shepherd will adapt to what he is trained to and will be better off with a regular routine.

You will find that without wearing a wristwatch, he will soon be telling time and reminding you that it is time for dinner, breakfast, a walk, or to go out. If you are not disposed to keeping a tight routine, you might want to train yourself, or just listen to your German Shepherd as he trains you.

Eating is another matter where routine is good for his digestion and for your schedule. Most breeders will recommend feeding the German Shepherd

Helpful Hints

Housetraining for a German Shepherd is usually a short task. In a couple of days he will get the message and want to return to his chosen spot to relieve himself. Regression in training is usually because he cannot get out to his spot in time. Giving him quick access to outside is usually the key to housetraining. His ability to retain will grow as he gets older, but for the first part of puppyhood he will need your help and thoughtfulness in getting to his spot quickly.

twice a day, usually first thing in the morning and then about the same time as your evening meal. Your puppy will not have the benefit of your schedule knowledge. He will not know that on one night a week, Suzie's soccer practice does not permit dinner until later. He will not know that your part-time job alters the schedule three mornings a week. His body will not consult the calendar to see when dinner is today; it will just start needing food.

So it is best, if at all possible, to be consistent and regular with his meals. The eating schedule will also play into his potty schedule, and if either one is disrupted, the other will be affected.

Our modern lifestyle has altered our human biology to be more random than prior generations who worked the farm and planned meals following the family work. Your German Shepherd can learn to accommodate some disruption of his routines, but he is best suited to as much regularity as you can provide.

Schedule No-No's

Some early studies on bloat and torsion showed a greater risk when dogs were fed once a day, fed from an elevated dish, and fed before or after vigorous exercise. Although we still do not know precisely the cause of these terrible events, it is wise to follow those cautions.

Feeding twice a day does help in the more frequent elimination of waste and in the control of stomach acid and digestion. As in the human cycles of schedule, vigorous exercise right before or after eating is uncomfortable and not recommended. Similarly, vigorous exercise right after a nap might be uncomfortable. To a large extent you can transfer your knowledge about yourself and your habit patterns to your German Shepherd. What is usually uncomfortable for you is probably not comfortable for him.

If you forget, or your schedule takes you away from his routine, there may be consequences. If he potties in the house because he was left inside for too long a period of time, disciplining him is not in order. You may also find a regression of his training and the need to retrain for a time until he is a little older. As he grows older, his routine will settle in and he will be more comfortable with it.

Grooming

Grooming will be covered in detail in Chapter 8. Yet, living with your German Shepherd has to do with your need to do for him what he cannot do for himself. So here are some grooming basics.

A soft-bristle brush is a good instrument for both removing loose hair and for giving attention to the dog. Most German Shepherds will love their grooming time. After brushing him with the grain of the coat and getting out what loose hair you can, you might want to brush easily against the grain to finish off the brushing. Many show dogs are prepared for the ring by brushing against the grain to fluff up the parts that may need to be enhanced

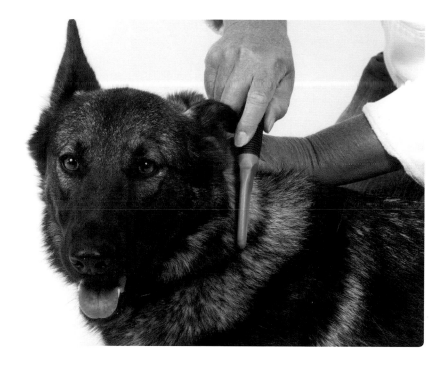

or emphasized. There are few things prettier than a well-groomed German Shepherd.

We have already talked about nails, but this is usually a more stressful matter the first few times. The puppy is certain that you are going to cut his paws off and feed them to the lions. He may struggle and flail about and try to get away. Violence is never a good idea with a dog, but if you wait for his permission to trim his nails, they may never get trimmed. So go ahead and get it done.

One way to do the nails is to stand over him and raise one foot at a time, back on the wrist, and upward so the toe is exposed but not uncomfortable and then just clip off the end of the nail. Another technique is to get him to lie down so you can get the proper angle to do the work. After a few times you will find him more at ease, knowing that although he may not like it much, it doesn't hurt and he will not die.

Cleaning the ears is also one of those things that may take a few times before he "gets it." Most ear infections involve moisture in the ear, so using water may

Breed Needs

Puppy Grooming Supplies

Keep these items readily available for grooming your puppy:

- ✔ Soft-bristle brush
- ✔ Dog nail clippers (appropriate size)
- ✔ Cotton balls
- ✔ Ear-cleaning solution
- ✔ Soft toothbrush
- ✔ Toothpaste for dogs
- ✔ Healthful treats

not be the best solution. Some people use rubbing alcohol, but that will also dry out the ears and can cause problems to the sensitive ear. There are ear solutions at most pet stores and veterinary offices that are prepared for this purpose. Most of them are a combination of rubbing alcohol, hydrogen peroxide *(peroxide should be used with caution in the ears)*, and water. Some will also include boric acid. Check with your veterinarian and then clean the ears regularly as part of your grooming routine. Dampen a cotton ball or washcloth with the solution and lightly wipe the inner surface of the ear, dragging the cloth toward you and out. For those tough folds in the ear, a simple cotton swab dampened with your solution should clean them up fine. If your dog begins to shake his head, rub his ear, or dig at it, you might try squirting one of the ear preparations into the ear, rub it around lightly to make sure it gets down inside, and then let him shake it out until it is dried. You might want to do this procedure outside.

When bathing your dog, finding a good place outside is most often wise. Depending on the weather, bathing outside will result in less cleanup on your part. Use a mild shampoo or a dog shampoo. The technique is up to you. It will work best if he is on a leash and if you have someone else hold him while you do the soaping. Simply wet the dog, apply the shampoo lightly, rub in, rinse out thoroughly, and let him shake.

The use of a dog dryer will quicken the task if you have one, or if the weather permits, he will dry in time. Dogs can suffer from the cold just as we do, so if you would be uncomfortable, he probably will be too. And, remember…a wet dog will prefer to jump on your bed and rub off on your covers, so close the door to any room in the house where you do not want him to go. Be sure to dry him thoroughly in cold temperatures or when it

is hot outside. A wet undercoat will retain heat or attract cold. In these temperature extremes be sure to dry him thoroughly to the touch.

Other than those basics, the German Shepherd is pretty much a wash-and-wear dog. German Shepherds do not require a lot of grooming or special coat care compared with some long-haired dogs. Regular brushing and regular exercise are necessary along with the occasional bath.

Teeth

Brushing your dog's teeth is similar to brushing your own, except he will probably not like your tooth paste and you will probably not like his. Remember, he cannot spit, and some ingredients in human toothpaste are toxic to dogs. There are other ways to clean his teeth other than brushing, but it needs to be done as part of your grooming routine. Be sure to get a regular assessment of his dental condition from your veterinarian and a cleaning if necessary. Your veterinarian will be able to look for gum disease and broken teeth. These conditions should not be ignored.

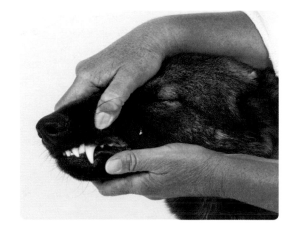

Chewing on a bone serves to help clean teeth, but not all bones are safe for dogs. Of course chicken bones are notoriously dangerous because they can splinter and have sharp points and edges. This is also true, however, for some other bones, including some beef bones, particularly after being cooked. Knuckle bones tend to be safer as do large rib bones that are not cooked until brittle. Marrow bones and round bones tend to be a delightful treat and are not typically in danger of splintering. However, pork bones, much like chicken bones, are to be avoided. Carrots can serve the purpose of cleaning the teeth and most dogs love to gnaw on a large carrot.

Somewhere between three and four months the puppy will start losing his baby teeth and begin to grow his adult set. During this time he will be chewing on anything and everything because of the soreness of his gums. Providing something safe for him to chew on is a good thing to do. There are teething bones available from your veterinarian or pet supply store, but a carrot or a beef bone can also help. Be careful of bones that splinter, such as chicken bones, pork bones, or smaller beef bones. Those splinters can cause serious injury to his digestive tract.

The teeth on each side of the lower jaw (mandible) start with three molars, four premolars, one canine and then the incisors (three on each side). The teeth on each side of the upper jaw (maxilla) start in the back with two molars, four premolars, one canine, and then three incisors. In a full mouth this is 42 total permanent teeth.

Missing or crooked teeth in the German Shepherd may not affect his health or suitability as a pet but are considered a serious fault in conformation shows. Missing teeth are considered a genetic trait.

Ears

The German Shepherd's ears may differ from line to line, but are usually up by one year of age. They will go through stages, from down as a little puppy to up for a while; they may go down again while the puppy is teething at about four to five months, then come back up and lean over in a tent fashion for a few weeks. But in most cases they will come up on their own. If, by the time the adult teeth are in, the ears are down at the base and not showing signs of coming up, it would be good to give them some help.

Taping the ears in place is a common practice for most breeders when they find a dog with weak ears. There are many techniques to accomplish this. Some veterinarians are accustomed to taping the ears of other breeds after cropping, yet some of those techniques involve an uncomfortable amount of tape and limit head and jaw mobility. Most breeders use a more subtle method, from a drop of Super Glue on the inside edge of each ear, gluing the edges of the ears together, to gluing a segment of pipe insulation inside the ear after cutting it to the ear's shape. Some also use pink foam hair curlers or other rounded lightweight foam products.

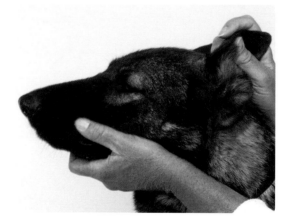

There are a variety of methods, but all involve setting the ear in an upright form to allow the crease of the down ear to strengthen and hold the ear upright. Check with your breeder or veterinarian for their advice.

Socialization

Socialization is an essential part of your German Shepherd's growth and training. As much as possible, take him into as many different environments as possible. Some few German Shepherds will be susceptible to stomach upset when riding in the car, and most young puppies will for a while. But short, regular rides will help to build confidence, and before long he will love to go in the car.

There are many places that will not allow dogs. Grocery stores and restaurants are usually off limits by health ordinance. One veterinarian conjectures that there are 11 diseases that are transmittable from dog to human, more than 100 that are transmittable from cat to human, and thousands that are communicable from human to human. So in the interest of public health, people should stay out of stores and restaurants, and dogs should be allowed in. But then, whether the threat is real or imagined, dogs are not always welcomed.

Taking him for walks where people are is a good way to expose him to our human world. Most people will welcome meeting a good dog, but not all. Some people are afraid and will avoid him, so be careful to avoid placing him in a position where he is frightened or picks up on the fear of others. Uncertain situations are fine as long as you are in control of him and the situation.

Parks are a great place for him to play and to meet people, but be careful of other pets. The German Shepherd is protective and territorial and may show some dog aggression. Although it is good to deal with that so he can go with you into any circumstances, turning him loose in a dog park might not be the first and best way to socialize him.

Dog parks are an admirable accommodation of certain communities for our animal-loving population, but they can also be places where irresponsible owners set up unexpected encounters that are not in your German Shepherd's best interest. Remember, he is territorial and he is a protector. Although some breeds may interpret the bounding, happy dog as a potential friend to play with, the German Shepherd may interpret him as a threat to his master's safety. If you are inclined to go to a dog park, it might be best to keep him on lead, at least until you are sure he is comfortable with the different behavior of the other breeds and people and can safely venture into the mix.

Puppy Training Classes
(Be sure your pup is current on all vaccinations.)
Training classes are another great place to socialize. These are usually controlled environments where he can interact with people and other dogs with a focus of something all are doing together. Your German Shepherd will love his training times and will try his best to please you.

Most communities have some resource for puppy training classes. Some city or county recreation departments sponsor training classes as well as some of the major pet store chains. Some communities have obedience clubs and offer training for puppies as well as continued training for adults through competitive titles. Check with your regional German Shepherd Dog club to see what they offer and what they recommend in your area.

Finding the right training for your puppy is important. You may want to choose your training class based on what job you have chosen for you and your German Shepherd. If you intend to go toward herding, agility, or obedience, then most training classes will get you started in the right direction. If you are interested in schutzhund, then starting your puppy early in this discipline is a good idea. Most schutzhund instructors will have you doing certain play exercises regularly throughout the day. Not all dogs are high drive enough for this sport, so contact a nearby club and get yours tested before you begin. If he is not suited to this activity, then it is best to not force him into it.

Conformation is one of the more difficult of competitions at which to excel. Conformation involves the dog being judged against the standard for his temperament, structure, and movement. It is exacting, and there is little training that can be done to improve the dog's chances of winning. Excellence in the conformation ring is largely a matter of the dog's breeding, not his training. This sport is quite popular and yet, unlike most other competitions, the winner gets the ribbons and the points and all the other dogs go home with nothing. So if your German Shepherd has the structure, temperament, and movement to excel, you will probably enjoy this competition. Many try it and then go on to other things if they do not win.

If you have a competitive conformation German Shepherd, you will want to start your puppy in training with the advice of a seasoned conformation person. There are certain obedience elements that you will not want your puppy doing. For instance, the conformation German Shepherd will always be moving out in front of the handler rather than heeling. He will also not sit when the handler stops, but will stand in his natural stack.

The German Shepherd stack has to do with how he naturally stands. In show competition, most dog breeds will stand foursquare, with both front and rear feet opposite from each other. With the German Shepherd, the natural stance is with one rear foot in front of the other more like a sprinter in the starting blocks, ready for the sprint.

Helpful Hints

Teaching your German Shepherd to go potty on command is a helpful practice when traveling. This can be accomplished by praising him when he goes, and then, when traveling, tell him to "go potty," or whatever term you use for this event, when you stop. The key is to stop at regular intervals and at times to coincide with his potty schedule. This way you can find a convenient place without any unplanned emergencies.

Travel with a German Shepherd

Your German Shepherd will love to travel with you. Hiking, fishing, boating, or just traveling is a great delight for him. He can accommodate long times in the car as long as he has regular potty breaks and exercise stops. There are even travel guides for people traveling with dogs, showing motels that are dog friendly and places to go with him at destination locations. You may want relief from the dog at your side all the time, but your German Shepherd will never tire of being at your side. He will go with you wherever you go and whenever you go.

BE PREPARED! German Shepherds on the Go

When traveling with your German Shepherd, make sure you bring everything you will need for the journey:

Crate: If you are flying, airlines will not accept a German Shepherd without a crate, usually a 500 size. Check with the airlines for regulations. If you are driving, this makes a safe place for him to travel and to sleep.

Collar, leash, and ID tag: He should be on leash at all times away from home, except in his crate.

Food: Find an appropriate plastic container for his regular food so he is not changing his diet while traveling.

Water: Changing his water supply on the road can be disastrous, so carry his regular water with you. (Freeze water in a bowl or container to provide a spill-proof source during travel, especially air travel.)

Toys: Take along his favorite toys. These can relieve boredom and also provide comfort.

Treats: Take along his favorite treats. You will want to reward him for his good travel behavior.

Dog bed: Like people, he will want to sleep on his own pad or blankets.

Medications: Be sure to take any prescription medications along plus his first aid kit.

Certificates: Take his vaccination records and registration papers or copies. Some jurisdictions are getting really strict about enforcing anti-dog laws. You can minimize some problems by having his papers with you.

Waste bags: Be sure to carry an ample supply of plastic bags to pick up his waste. This will assure that you are welcome back on your next trip.

Air travel is a particular challenge and is becoming harder as time goes on. That is not because the dogs do not like to go but because of changes in airline policies. Some airlines will no longer take dogs, and those that will have increased their prices substantially. For the German Shepherd, most airlines require a size 500 crate, but few airplanes can get a 500 crate through the cargo doors. So be sure, before you show up at the gate with your dog, that you have checked with the airline for the following information:

- Whether they take dogs
- What size crate they require
- If the specific plane you are flying on can take the required crate
- What the price is both ways
- Whether there are layovers and plane changes for the dog

Increasingly, airlines are downsizing their aircraft to reduce costs per mile and to ensure a full passenger load. This also reduces the cargo space and in

Helpful Hints

There are a number of websites that provide travel information for dog lovers:

Pets Welcome
www.petswelcome.com

Official Pet Hotels
www.officialpethotels.com

Dog Friendly
www.dogfriendly.com

Travel Pets
www.travelpets.com

many cases decreases the access-door sizes to the cargo hold. In doing so, the airlines are less able to handle larger dogs and crates. Before you travel on an airline, be sure to determine which aircraft you will be on and whether that particular aircraft can take your crate. Not all ticket agents will know this information, so be sure to make contact with the right department and person who can guarantee you that your German Shepherd can fly with you.

All of these things will affect the quality of the travel experience and the stress on your dog.

Probably the most important advice for traveling with dogs is the ever present plastic bag. Restrictions on dogs along tourist routes have come about because of dog owners who do not pick up after their dogs. It is not a great inconvenience to carry some plastic bags large enough to contain their waste and to simply insert your hand into the bag, lean over and pick up the doggy poop and then invert the bag back over your hand. In this way, the hand is never soiled and the bag is clean on the outside. If every dog owner did this, we would all be welcomed at far more places.

A German Shepherd Is a Dog!

With all of his superior intelligence, attention to your world, and sensitivity, it is easy to forget that he is, after all, a dog. He will, however, remind you regularly. He will bark, urinate while on your walk in an inappropriate place, sniff a visitor in an inappropriate place, or bring you something dead. He will embarrass you without feeling the least embarrassed himself, for his behavior is appropriate in his dog world if not in yours.

Barking

The German Shepherd is not usually a nonstop barker as some breeds tend to be. He will usually bark at a specific object that he considers a threat or to which he feels the need to draw attention. Where that is inappropriate, you will need to train him to stop. A simple voice command with repetition will usually do the trick. Be careful, however, that you investigate to make sure it is inappropriate and not something you should have paid attention to.

Biting

Your German Shepherd does not have fingers as we do, so his mouth is his primary way of feeling things. He will bite to feel, bite to play, and bite to eat. In fact, for the first few months he will want to bite a lot. The problem is, he will have very sharp teeth and will not have developed a sense of how strong his bite is. You will have to help him understand what he can and cannot bite, when he can and cannot bite, and when he must stop. Verbal commands are usually the most effective, but sometimes a light finger flicked on the nose can help. Again, the puppy is vulnerable to injury just as a child is, so anger and violence are never appropriate. The objective is to teach the command or to reinforce the command only.

Aggressive Behavior

The German Shepherd is naturally protective and can become aggressive if trained to do so or if not trained how and when to express his protective behavior. This training should begin at an early age and continue so that he is a good citizen and can be around people without being a threat.

A German Shepherd should never be trained to be aggressive except in encouraging his play drive and focusing it in police training, military training, and the schutzhund sports. These activities are never intended to make him mean but to focus his play drive into a disciplined sport or service activity. The German Shepherd should never be trained to "sic 'em" when it comes to people or other animals. His protective nature is adequate to make him the guardian he was bred to be. It is that nature that needs to be focused and disciplined.

Chewing

Puppies chew. It is good to understand that your puppy's genetics and nature cause him to chew and that if you try to stop him from chewing anything, you will create conflict. It is very frustrating for the puppy when God is saying "chew" and your master is saying "no." But it is not appropriate to chew on anything and everything, so provide him with a rope toy or something indestructible on which he can chew. An old worn-out shoe is usually a good item, but he will have to learn which shoe is his and which shoes are not.

There are many items made for puppies to chew on, but some are not safe. Many veterinarians recommend against rawhide chew bones, sticks, and other rawhide items. If swallowed, they can absorb moisture, swell up, and become impassable, requiring surgery to remove them. Check with your veterinarian if you have any concerns or need recommendations.

Other cautions include hard rubber balls with one hole in them. There have been incidents of dogs chomping down on them, creating a vacuum, and getting their tongue stuck in the hole. There are other toys that are advertised as indestructible that the German Shepherd can destroy and swallow. Find something for him to chew on, but use careful judgment in selecting what that will be. Chewing will last through the loss of puppy teeth and the growth of new adult teeth, and then it will not be such an issue.

Digging

Dogs dig. They have nails for digging. They dig up things and dig holes in which to hide things. They dig dens to live in and holes in which to lie down. If you have a yard that is more important than your dog, you might want to consider a statue of a dog. If you have a German Shepherd, he will not be as bad as a terrier that is bred to hunt varmints or as bad as some of the other earth hunters, but he will dig.

You may want to reinforce where your fence contacts the ground if your German Shepherd starts digging out, but more than likely, he will just dig randomly within his yard to hide a bone or to explore a smell or to make a cool place to lie down. Providing discipline and direction for this behavior may be necessary in your setting, but another approach is to find joy in surveying his yard with a hole here and there, scattered toys, and the ever present remaining part of his knuckle bone. To some degree, this is all part of sharing your life and property with your German Shepherd.

Escaping

Some German Shepherds accept their confinement easily and never challenge their fence. Some, however, are not content to know what is in the yard but must explore the world around them. They cannot be permitted this privilege. For those escape artists, your competitive spirit will have to rise to the level of his escape activity, and you will need to win, providing for confinement.

Disaster Preparedness

If you live in an area where natural disasters are possible, you probably already have a disaster plan for your family. Now that you have a new member of the family, you should revise your plan to include him. Having a supply of food and water for him in case of a flood or hurricane is as essential as having your own supplies.

Having a first aid kit handy is also a good idea. Although your family first aid kit may have some of the supplies you need, it will certainly not have everything that you might need for your dog. *(See First Aid Section page 98.)*

Here are some of the items you might consider storing in his kit:

- Gauze pads—50 4-by-4-inch (10-by-10-cm) sponges, two per envelope
- Triple antibiotic ointment
- Rubbing alcohol
- Charcoal tablets or powder
- Ear syringe—2-ounce (60-mL) capacity
- Ace self-adhering athletic bandage—3-inch (8-cm) width
- White petroleum jelly (Vaseline or similar)
- Eye wash
- Sterile, nonadhesive pads
- Pepto Bismol tablets
- Generic Benadryl capsules—25 mg, for allergies
- Hydrocortisone acetate —1 percent cream
- Sterile stretch gauze bandage—3 inches by 4 yards (8 cm by 3.6 m)
- Buffered aspirin
- Dermicil hypoallergenic cloth tape—1 inch by 10 yards (2.5 cm by 9 m)
- Hydrogen peroxide
- Kaopectate tablets, maximum strength
- Bandage scissors
- Custom splints
- Veterinary stretch bandage
- Blanket
- Tweezers
- Muzzle
- Hemostats
- Rectal thermometer
- Ziplock bags
- Paperwork, including the dog's health record, medications, local and national poison-control numbers, regular veterinary clinic hours and telephone numbers, and emergency clinic hours and telephone number.

Just as with children, your dog will step on something, investigate a critter he shouldn't have, play too hard, or eat something that is not good for him. Being prepared beforehand can save his life. Finding out what to do in case of a poisoning, a snakebite, or other health emergencies is worthwhile before the emergency arrives.

Communicating with Your German Shepherd

Voice

You will find your German Shepherd attentive to your voice. He will listen for words he has become accustomed to and those he understands. Using sentences will not confuse him as he selects from those sentences words he understands. For training, you will want to use single word commands that have obedient action expectations attached to them, but in general "off-training" times, he loves to have you talk to him. He will listen not only for words that he understands (*walk*, *ride*, *go*, etc.) but to the tone, and the inflections that communicate the emotion of the moment. Shouting does not work well, in that it will tend to drive him away. He may know that you are displeased, but he will also sense danger and retreat from it. It is better to communicate your displeasure in emphatic tones while shaking a finger. If he senses your displeasure without a threat, he will listen and attempt to understand. He will enjoy your being happy and pleased and will respond with his own joy and pleasure. Enthusiastic higher-pitched speech will tell him you are happy and playful.

Hands

The German Shepherd is quite adept at learning hand signals. Most military and police training involves teaching hand signals so that the sounds of the commands are not heard by the enemy or suspect. This part of the training is rather simple and easy. Simply use the hand signal with the accompanying word to communicate the desired response. He will learn them together in the obedience training so you do not have to go through two steps. There are a number of Internet websites that show hand signals for dog training.

Facial Expressions

The German Shepherd will naturally learn your facial expressions. He is far more observant of the details of movement and expression than we humans are. He will notice your smile, frown, a questioning look, and a stern appearance. Given just a little time he will know what is going on with you and even sense what you are feeling and thinking. While you might want to emphasize something to him by overdramatizing with your facial expressions, it is largely unnecessary, as he will read you quite well without your having to train him to do so. Conversely it is important to learn his facial expressions. You will notice differences in his eyes, the set and tilt of the ears, the carriage of the head up or down, and the set of the mouth, tongue, and jaw. Just as we betray our emotions with our facial expressions, so does the German Shepherd.

Body Movements

The German Shepherd will learn to read your body movement also. He will see the movement of your hands, arms, and shoulders and will learn to know when you are coming to him, leaving, tired, excited, and all that is communicated by body language. He will also give you body movement clues as to what is going on in his head. The hung head in the presence of the trash on the floor may mean, "Who, me? I have no clue who was in the trash!" The tail is also a dead giveaway. The raised tail is a sign of dominance when approaching another person or animal, whereas the tail held down is a sign of submission. Prancing at the door means.... Well, you get the idea.

Scents

Whereas we identify other people and animals by sight, the German Shepherd will identify them by scent—his primary sense. It is believed by many that even our emotions can trigger biological and chemical changes in our scent and that dogs can literally smell fear, anger, or other human emotions. What we do know about his keen sense of smell is that he can smell things that we cannot and will smell things far sooner than we will. When his nose is to the ground, or in the air, he is on the trail of something. His instinct is to track it down and investigate what he has discovered with his nose. Tracking training is to some degree training the dog to move through a maze of scents toward the desired objective; the other part of the training is teaching the handler to trust the dog's scenting ability.

Chapter Six

Health and Nutrition

From his very first checkup to his last senior checkup, your German Shepherd will be depending on you for his health care and his nutrition. Not all foods are equal, and not all veterinarians are equal. Making those choices is very important for your new friend.

German Shepherds are hearty and active dogs that require the proper amounts of protein, carbohydrates, and vitamins and minerals. Some argue that the dog in the wild survived on anything and everything in pre-history; so did the caveman. We also know that the life span of both human and animal with modern nutrition has increased dramatically and that many diseases of the past are no longer an issue because our knowledge of nutrition and medical care has increased dramatically. Besides, the domesticated dog is as far from the wild dog as the caveman is from modern humans. Whether all the changes we have made are progress or not is debatable, but we have learned a lot about nutrition, and the advances in medicine are nothing short of phenomenal. Applying that progress to our German Shepherd is an essential point of responsibility in our having him for our pet and companion.

Finding the Right Veterinarian

You may already have a veterinarian you trust because you have other pets or have had them in the past. It is not necessary to change veterinarians. But if you do not have an established relationship with a veterinarian, it is best to start that relationship early in your dog's life. He will need to have his full set of puppy shots and rabies shots early. So find a good veterinarian who understands your breed at the very start.

You will want to find a veterinarian who understands German Shepherds both in temperament and in terms of their particular health issues. Your breeder may be able to help direct you and to avoid some of the pitfalls that others have experienced. All breeds of dogs have a core set of health issues that are part of the breed genetics. Finding someone who understands those issues for the German Shepherd is your best bet, if you can.

Some veterinarians will not like your German Shepherd or will be afraid of him. Others simply have no experience with the breed. Breed-specific experience might at some point be crucial in understanding a problem you encounter. Again, having a good relationship with your breeder will also be of value in that sometimes breeders know things about the breed that an inexperienced veterinarian may not understand. Your breeder is not a veterinarian and should not replace the experience and education of a veterinarian, but if they have been breeding for any length of time, they probably have experienced every problem the breed presents. This experience can be of great value in providing high-quality care for your new friend.

There are some old wives' tales and fables that are believed by the general public that are simply not true. Unfortunately those untruths are sometimes believed by a few veterinarians. Although some interpret the angles of the German Shepherd's structure as an indication of hip problems, the fact is there is no correlation. Statistics show a general trend of improvement over the past 40 years that is undeniable. The historic hip problem in this breed, although part of its genetic heritage, has been vigorously addressed by German Shepherd breeders and is now no longer its number one problem.

Another trend of the past was the palpation of hips. In the early 1970s there was a fad going around that involved feeling (palpating) the hips and diagnosing problems by that method. Litters across the nation were put down because of the subjective "feeling" of mostly well-meaning veterinarians who were trained in this technique. The fact is, hip problems are rarer today than ever before and can be diagnosed only by a good radiograph read by a competent radiologist or specialist. Unless your veterinarian has X-ray vision, he or she should rely on the actual X-ray film to diagnose a hip problem.

It is reasonably established that hip dysplasia is a genetic problem, so the solution is to not breed those dogs who have it. There are treatments that can alleviate the pain

Breed Truths

It is not unusual for people to comment on the stride of the German Shepherd and ask, "What's wrong with your dog's rear end?" The fact is that the hip problems of past years have been largely addressed by careful breeders, but the history and rumors remain. This same reaction can also be found in some veterinarians who have not kept up with this progress. When getting an assessment of the German Shepherd's rear structure and movement, always ask for an X-ray and do not accept an observation as though the doctor has X-ray vision. You cannot know what is going on inside the hip unless you can see inside the hip. The German Shepherd gate is supposed to be different from any other breed—more horizontal and catlike than "short and vertical" like most dog breeds.

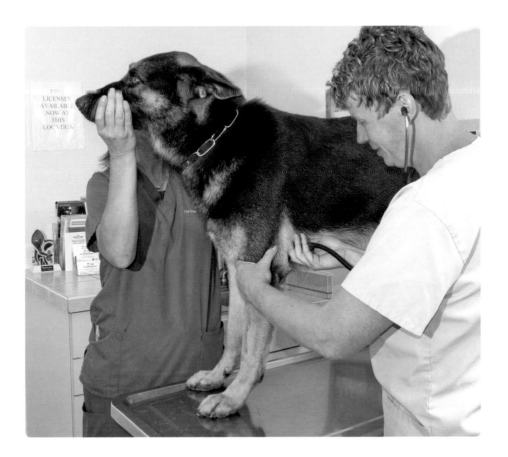

a dog might suffer from this condition. Adequan Canine polysulfated gly-cosaminoglycan (PSGAG) is a product used both to control the symptoms and to alter the underlying degenerative disease process of canine arthritis. Adequan Canine is a member of a new class of drugs termed disease-modi-fying osteoarthritis drugs (DMOAD). It is a therapy to control the pain and inflammation of canine arthritis. Although it works to affect the cartilage of the joint, it cannot re-form a joint that is genetically deformed. The best solu-tion to canine hip dysplasia is to breed away from it by using proper breed-ing tools.

There is other folklore about German Shepherds and their health and nature that is baseless. You may hear that German Shepherds with a black spot on their tongue have come from a line mixed with a chow. The fact is that many German Shepherds have a black spot on their tongue and it is not a defect or against the standard, and it does not make them related to another breed.

Interviewing a few veterinarians before choosing is not any more unrea-sonable than interviewing doctors before choosing one for yourself. It will be a good time to ask them about their experience with the breed and what breed-specific health issues they would be concerned about. It is also not unreasonable to take that information back to your breeder to cross-check and see if this veterinarian is predisposed to old folklore or is truly an experienced scientist. Your German Shepherd's life may ultimately depend on it.

The First Checkup

Making the trip to the veterinarian is a terrifying experience for most dogs. You can help make it as positive an experience as it can be by doing some fun things. Giving a treat at each stage of the visit can help. Also, be careful that your own tensions and apprehensions are not being fed into the dog. It is common to say that the emotions of the owner go down the lead. It does seem to be true.

At the first checkup the veterinarian will usually check the puppy's eyes, ears, and feet, and push gently around on the abdomen. This is both to find any unusual hard spots or growths and to observe for any pain response from the dog. The veterinarian will also look inside the mouth and basically check the dog over from nose to tail, including listening to the heart and lungs.

The veterinarian will want to know if you have shot records from the breeder to incorporate into their records system and will recommend the shot regimen for your puppy's future as well as the frequency of health checks and recommended procedures. Depending on the environmental risks where you live, he may recommend continuous heartworm medications and other parasite controls. He may want you to bring a stool sample at regular intervals and to use worm medications appropriate to your area. These little items all combine to make for a healthy and happy dog.

Different areas of the country have different health issues. In some high, dry climates parasites and worms are virtually unheard of, whereas in lower elevations and damper, warmer climates, all kinds of microscopic organisms are a threat. There are some good Internet sites that can give you some tips on what to expect in your area, but most veterinarians will be familiar with the local issues.

Immunizations

Twenty years ago there were fewer identified diseases than there are today and the immunization protocol was simple: Every veterinarian used the same protocol. Today, studies have shown that certain vaccines protect for less than a year and some for far more than a year.

The problem has been that local immunization laws for pets required a rigid vaccination period. Over the years veterinary medicine has worked to modify those laws to better reflect the reality of vaccine coverage. Different vaccine producers also use different processes and their vaccines are recommended for different periods of time. So be sure to check with your veterinarian to see what products they supply and the frequency of administration that they recommend.

Most veterinarians will use a combined vaccine consisting of several "core vaccines" in one shot. They will usually cover canine distemper, canine parvovirus infection, adenovirus, parainfluenza, and canine hepatitis. Additional

BE PREPARED! Immunization Schedule

Each veterinarian will have an immunization schedule that he recommends. It may look something like this:

First Core Vaccination—6–8 weeks of age
Canine distemper, canine parvovirus infection, adenovirus, parainfluenza, and canine hepatitis.

Second Core Vaccination—10–12 weeks of age
The veterinarian may also add leptospirosis or Lyme disease vaccines if they are common in your area.

Third Core Vaccination—14–16 weeks of age
Rabies Vaccination—16–24 weeks of age

Annual core vaccine booster—1 year of age
Core vaccine booster every 1–3 years after the first year

"noncore vaccines," such as one for canine kennel cough (*Bordetella*), as well as other vaccines may be appropriate based on the pet's particular needs.

Rabies vaccination is often given as a separate shot, and the bordetella immunization may be given nasally. The American Veterinary Medical Association recommends that veterinarians customize vaccination programs to the needs of their patients. More than one vaccination program may be effective.

Heartworms are a serious threat in some parts of the country but are not a threat in drier, cooler climates. This infection is carried by mosquitoes and there is a simple test to determine if it is present. If the parasite is present in your area, it is good to provide the protection.

Kennel cough or *Bordetella* is highly contagious but usually not a serious infection and is transmitted from dog to dog. It is usually found in kennels, hence the common name, at dog shows, or at dog parks. If your German Shepherd travels with you and is around other animals, it is good to provide the available protection.

External Parasites

Fleas

Fleas thrive where the weather is warm and humid. Check with your veterinarian to see if fleas are a problem, and if so, whether they are a seasonal or year-round problem. Fleas can be picked up wherever an infestation exists, often in areas frequented by other cats and dogs. Adult fleas are usually dark brown, about the size of a sesame seed, and are able to move over your pet's skin rapidly.

The adult flea spends all of its time on your pet. Female fleas begin laying eggs within 24 hours of finding a host, producing as many as 50 eggs a day. These eggs will fall from your pet everywhere he goes, spreading the infestation. A small, wormlike larvae hatches from the eggs and attaches itself to carpets, furniture, or into soil and then begins spinning a cocoon. The cocooned flea pupae can survive as a dormant creature for weeks before emerging as an adult, ready to infest (or reinfest) your German Shepherd. Fleas live from six weeks to six months and can literally take over the environment in which your German Shepherd lives.

Treatment and Control Ask your veterinarian to recommend a good flea control for him based on your needs, your pet's needs, and the severity of the flea infestation.

Since most of the flea's life cycle is spent off your pet, treating him will not eliminate the problem. You have to kill the adult fleas and the eggs, larvae, and pupae, or your pet will become reinfested when these fleas become adults and the cycle starts all over again. Careful and regular vacuuming and cleaning of the pet's living area can help to remove and kill flea eggs, larvae, and pupae. There are also chemical treatments that can help, that are not toxic to your pet. These products may be available from a pest-control company, where carpet cleaning equipment is available for rent, or at the local supermarket. Be sure to consult with your veterinarian to see which products are safe for use around pets and children. Flea larvae are more resistant than adult fleas to insecticides. Your veterinarian can also recommend an appropriate course of action to prevent future flea infestations in your yard and home.

Ticks

There are many different species of ticks that can affect dogs and cats. Ticks are most often found in tall grass, brush, shrubs, and wild undergrowth. Experts disagree about their habitat. Some believe they live only in grass, and others believe they inhabit any organic plant in the wild. In any event, they travel easily from their natural environment to any host that comes into contact with them. This can be any animal or human that enters their environment. Immature ticks often feed on small birds or wild animals found in forests, prairies, and brush. Adult ticks seek larger hosts like dogs and cats that venture into these habitats. Tick exposure is usually seasonal, depending on your geographic location and temperature range.

Check your dog regularly for stickers and pests.

Feel through the coat for stickers, and if you find them, remove them and comb out any tangled hair.

You can check for fleas by rolling the dog onto his back and combing the underbelly with a fine-tooth flea comb.

To check for ticks, feel for lumps about your dog's body and behind the ears. If you find one, you can remove it by gently pulling on it until it releases. Make sure not to pull so hard that you pull the body off, leaving the head attached. If you do, be sure to remove the head with tweezers.

Ticks are usually found around your dog's neck, ears, and in the folds between the legs and the body. They can be found anywhere on the body and are usually easily seen or felt. An adult female tick can ingest up to 100 times her weight in blood! Ticks are also capable of spreading serious infectious diseases (such as Lyme disease, Rocky Mountain spotted fever, and others) to the pets and the people on which they feed. The diseases they carry vary by geographic area and the tick species.

Treatment and Control Remove ticks as soon as they are discovered. This is very important because it lessens the chance of disease transmission from the tick to your German Shepherd. To remove ticks use tweezers or firmly grip the tick as close to the pet's skin as possible and gently and steadily pull the tick free without twisting it or crushing it. You want to be careful to get the whole tick without breaking off the head, which can cause further infection. After removing the tick, dispose of it by crushing it while avoiding contact with the fluids, which carry disease. Do not attempt to apply a hot match to it or smother the tick with alcohol or petroleum jelly. This can cause the tick to regurgitate saliva into the wound and increase the risk of disease if it is infected.

Your veterinarian can recommend a product suited to your pet's needs. But also be sure his vaccinations are up to date. If you enjoy outdoor activities with your German Shepherd, such as camping, sporting, or hiking trips, you should examine him for ticks immediately upon returning home and remove them. Be sure to keep your yard grass cut low. It may be a good practice to spray shrubs and other plants with an appropriate insecticide during tick season. Also, if you were in tick areas or find a tick on your pet, be careful to inspect yourself and other family members also. Ticks are not necessarily species specific.

Ear Mites

Ear mites are also geographical in distribution, and are more frequent in moist, warm climates. They are more common in young cats and dogs, and generally found in the ears and surrounding area. Mites are tiny and can be seen only with a microscope. Infestation usually occurs by contact with another infected animal.

Ear mites cause irritation of the ear canal. Head shaking and scratching of the ears can be signs of ear mite infestation. Scratching can be so intense that it causes bleeding sores around the ears. A brown or black ear discharge is common with ear mites, and secondary infections with bacteria or yeast are common. An examination under a microscope can confirm the presence of ear mites.

Treatment and Control Treatment of ear mites involves regular ear cleaning and medication. Your veterinarian can provide an effective treatment plan.

Breed Truths

German Shepherd ears act as funnels for sound, making his hearing acute and focused. But they also act as funnels for dirt, stickers, sticks, and other debris. Be sure to check his ears regularly, particularly when he starts shaking his head or digging at the ear.

Sarcoptic Mange Mites

Microscopic sarcoptic mange mites cause sarcoptic mange, also known as scabies. Sarcoptic mange can affect dogs of all ages and sizes during any time of the year. Sarcoptic mange mites are highly contagious and may be passed by close contact with infected animals, bedding, or grooming tools.

Sarcoptic mange mites burrow into the top layer of the dog's skin and cause intense itching. Clinical signs include generalized hair loss, a skin rash, and crusting. Secondary infections and skin problems may also accompany the mange problem. People may develop a skin rash when they come in close contact with an affected dog and should seek medical attention. Sarcoptic mange is confirmed by examining a skin scraping under a microscope.

Treatment and Control Dogs with sarcoptic mange require medication to kill the mites and treatment to soothe the skin and resolve related infections. Cleaning and treating their environment is also necessary.

Demodectic Mange Mites

Demodectic mange mites are microscopic and not highly contagious. In general, demodex mites are not usually spread to other animals or across species. A mother dog, however, may pass the mites to her puppies.

Localized demodectic mange is more common in young dogs (usually less than six months old) and is seen as patches of scaly skin and redness around the eyes and mouth. Itching is not common with this type of mite infestation unless there is a secondary infection. Demodectic mange may signal an underlying medical condition, and the dog's overall health should be carefully evaluated. Less commonly, young and old dogs experience a more severe form of demodectic mange (generalized demodecosis) and can exhibit patches of redness, hair loss, and scaly, thickened skin. Dogs with this infestation can develop secondary bacterial infections of the skin that require additional treatment.

Demodectic mange is confirmed by taking a skin scraping and examining it under a microscope.

Treatment and Control There are several commercial preparations available that contain sulfated lime. Your veterinarian can prescribe topical applications and/or oral antibiotics. Puppies and young dogs are most vulnerable and often outgrow their vulnerability as their immune system matures.

General Precautions for External Parasites

Be sure to check your German Shepherd over regularly from head to tail and note any changes in habits or itching. When you suspect any kind of infestation, check it out and stop it early. The sooner you catch it and get it under control, the easier it will be on you and on him.

Wash his bedding regularly in hot water, using an appropriate mild detergent. Prevention is easier than doing battle with parasites after they have established their presence.

If your area is parasite prone, treating him and his environment with an appropriate preventive preparation is a good idea.

Internal Parasites

Most internal parasites are worms and single-celled organisms that can exist in the intestines of most dogs. The most common worms are hookworms, whipworms, roundworms, and tapeworms. These worms can be present in domestic animals or in many wild animals. They are usually passed on to other animals by their larvae's presence in their feces.

Common single-cell parasites are coccidia and *Giardia*.

Roundworms

Roundworms are the most common intestinal parasite in dogs in the world. Animals with roundworms pass the infection to other animals when the worm eggs develop into larvae and are present in the animal's feces (droppings). Your German Shepherd can pick up the infection by eating infected soil, licking contaminated fur or paws, or drinking contaminated water.

Although these worms are common in most areas of the world, they are more common in warm, humid climates. Dry, cold climates can hinder their development outside of their host. Infected female dogs may pass the infection to their puppies before birth or afterward when they are nursing.

Puppies are the usual victims of roundworm infection. Roundworms live in the small intestine and can steal nutrients from the food your pet eats, which can lead to malnutrition and intestinal problems.

Roundworm infections can be transmitted to humans. Most infections come from accidentally eating the worm larvae or from larvae that enter through the skin. For example, children may become infected if they play in areas that contain infected feces, such as in the dirt or in an unsanitary sandbox, and pick up the larvae on their hands.

Hookworms

Hookworms are the second most common intestinal parasites found in dogs. Your German Shepherd can become infected when larvae penetrate the animal's skin or the lining of the mouth. An infected female dog can pass the infection to her puppies in her milk.

Hookworms are dangerous parasites because they actually bite into the intestinal lining of an animal and suck blood. As with roundworms, puppies and kittens are at high risk of infection and developing severe diseases. Left untreated, hookworm infections can result in potentially life-threatening blood loss, weakness, and malnutrition.

Like roundworms, hookworm infections can be transmitted to humans by the larvae entering through the skin. The larvae produce severe itching and tunnel-like, red areas as they move through the skin, and should be treated as soon as discovered.

Whipworms

Whipworms get their name from their whiplike shape. Whipworms pass the infection along to other animals when the worm eggs develop into larvae and are passed in their feces. As with most other worm infections, your German Shepherd can pick up the infection by eating infected soil or licking his contaminated fur or paws.

Like hookworms, whipworms bury their heads in the lining of an animal's intestine and suck blood, but they usually do not cause health problems and are generally less harmful to their host. Rare, severe infections can develop and lead to diarrhea and weight loss. Whipworm larvae rarely infect humans when they are accidentally eaten.

Tapeworms

Tapeworms are so designated because they look like a piece of tape. They are thin and flat, like strips of tape. Unlike the uni-bodied roundworms, hookworms, and whipworms, tapeworms' bodies are made up of joined segments. Dogs usually become infected with tapeworms when they eat infected fleas or lice. Certain types of tapeworms are present in certain infected rodents and rabbits.

Tapeworms also live in the small intestine and steal the nutrients from the food your German Shepherd eats. The infection is usually discovered when the egg sacs are seen under the pet's tail around his anus or on his stool. These sacs look like flattened grains of rice. There are several de-wormers available that work well against tapeworms, but keeping your pet free of fleas is the best preventive. Tapeworms are not usually a risk to people.

General Precautions

If you notice a change in your pet's appetite or coat, diarrhea, or excessive coughing, see your veterinarian. It is a good practice to periodically take a fecal sample as soon as he goes potty and place it in a clean pill bottle or other container and take it to your veterinarian for microscopic observation. A fecal sample test can detect the presence of worm eggs or adults, and your veterinarian will recommend a de-worming medication. A good way to prevent worm infections is to use once-monthly heartworm preventives available from your veterinarian.

Nursing female dogs and their litters are major sources of the spread of infective eggs and larvae. If you are expecting a litter of puppies, be sure to consult your veterinarian early in the pregnancy and ask about a worming protocol.

CAUTION

Be sure your German Shepherd's water supply is protected from and not available to other wild animals and birds. Many internal and external parasites are carried to domestic pets from creatures of the wild, and coccidia and *Giardia* are often introduced to domestic pets through their water supply. If you choose to provide water and food for wild creatures, be sure that your pets cannot access it.

Worm infections in humans are rare and can easily be prevented by practicing good hygiene and sanitation. Picking up early and regularly after your German Shepherd will help to eliminate the risk to children at play with him. Children should not eat dirt and should limit their play to areas where pet feces is not common. Your German Shepherd will choose an area of the yard as his toilet, and it is best to play elsewhere. Sandboxes should be covered when not in use, as stray cats may be attracted to them. Adults and children should always wash their hands after handling dirt. Dog feces should be immediately picked up from public areas. A good German Shepherd owner will always have a supply of plastic bags large enough to accomplish this task. The process is simple and easy. Simply place your hand in the bag, reach down and pick up the feces, and then invert the bag over the hand with the feces now in the bottom of the inverted bag. Then tie or secure the bag and dispose of it in the trash.

An empty pill bottle, rinsed with clear water, makes an excellent container for a small drop of fecal material to carry to the veterinarian's office for analysis. This can be stored in the refrigerator safely and without contamination until it is brought in for analysis.

Coccidia

Coccidia are single-celled parasites and can be observed only through a microscope. Your pet can become infected by eating infected soil, drinking contaminated water, or licking contaminated paws or fur. Once swallowed, the parasites multiply, damaging the lining of the intestine, and your pet cannot absorb nutrients from its food. Bloody, watery diarrhea may result, and he may become dehydrated because he loses more water in his stool than he can replace by drinking. Young German Shepherds are often infected because their immune systems are not yet strong enough to fight off the parasite. Coccidia can be very contagious among young puppies, so households with multiple pets should be careful to practice good hygiene and sanitation. Clean water is a good step in prevention, and keeping the water where birds cannot get into it is also wise.

A regular fecal test by your veterinarian can detect the presence of coccidia. Treatment with medications will prevent the parasite from multiplying and allow time for your pet's immune system to kill it.

Giardia

Giardia is also a single-celled parasite that, when swallowed, multiplies and damages the lining of the intestine, reducing the absorption of nutrients from the food your German Shepherd eats. Although most *Giardia* infections do not cause other illnesses, severe infections can lead to diarrhea.

Giardia is harder to diagnose than other intestinal parasites, and may require repeated stool samples to confirm its presence. This infection is often called "Beaver Fever" because of its being found in places where rodents frequent water sources. Keeping your dog's water supply fresh and clean is one good step in preventing *Giardia*. Your veterinarian can recommend a treatment with medications to eliminate the infection. Because it is highly contagious among animals, good hygiene and sanitation are essential when there are multiple pets in the household.

Allergies and Skin Problems

The German Shepherd, like almost all dog breeds, can be allergic to various and sundry chemicals, plants, and foods. For the comfort of your German Shepherd it is good to be aware of any rashes or breaking out, usually found around the belly or other areas where you can observe the skin. Although some lines may tend to have greater allergic reactions than others, by and large the German Shepherd is not allergy prone.

Food allergies are usually detected by the presence of a rash or by diarrhea. Some of the more common allergies are to certain grains, like wheat or corn, and to chicken-based foods. Many dog food manufacturers include chicken parts, which may include feathers and other items that your dog's digestive system simply cannot tolerate. If you suspect a food allergy, try switching the food, buying a smaller bag until you can see how the switch has affected the problem. It may take several "switches" before you find the right diet for him. If this does not eliminate the problem in short order, consult with your veterinarian to see if there may be some other health issue.

German Shepherd Health Issues

Every breed has its own set of health issues that are common and specific to the breed. The German Shepherd is no exception. Learning the issues of the past, although they may not be major issues of the present, will help to keep them nonissues in breeding future generations of healthy animals.

Because German Shepherds have been separated into various camps and bred for different purposes, their health issues may be more than breed specific. They may be related to the breeding program and general function for which the dogs were bred. American-bred German Shepherds and German-bred German Shepherds (import lines) all come from the same

original gene pool, but the differences in their breeding objective and purpose have given them some distinct health issues. Some genetic diseases are present in certain lines but not in others. If your breeder is not familiar with those differences, seek out your regional breed club and find the most knowledgeable person in that club you can find. They can be a valuable resource in setting up your health care plan.

Taking Your German Shepherd to Work!

There are many jobs and companies where dogs are permitted to go with their owners to work. If you are fortunate to have such a work situation, by all means take him. The German Shepherd needs a job and will adapt quite well to most work environments. In addition to their traditional roles as guardians in police work and the military, they have been used as therapy dogs, as couriers, and as a variety of helpers. At least one German Shepherd accompanied a pastor to church, sitting at his side during the sermon.

The use of hip certifications has largely reduced the incidents of hip dysplasia in the breed in general, although most reputable breeders still will not breed without a certification or some indication from a competent veterinarian that their breeding stock is without significant breeding risk.

Fortunately, we have many more tools in finding and dealing with health problems than ever before. The Orthopedic Foundation for Animals (OFA) has health statistics available on their website—*http://www.offa.org/ stats.html*—that can be a guide in monitoring your German Shepherd and in your future breeding plans. It is better to have the scientific facts than to rely on rumors.

First Aid for Your German Shepherd

You now have a first aid kit and a relationship with a good veterinarian and you are ready. Sure enough, you will need all of this and a bit more when the emergency inevitably comes. It might be a good idea to find another dog owner and talk through various possibilities before the emergency arrives so that you will have some plan and training on how to act rather than panic.

Dehydration

Dehydration is one of the most common and dangerous health issues for a dog, particularly for an active athlete like the German Shepherd. Vigorous exercise in sporting events or running and hiking can deplete the body's moisture supply and create more serious problems.

The usual activities of a sport or of play in the wilderness should be accompanied by adequate supplies of water. The greater the physical exertion the more water intake should be encouraged and available. This is equally true for normal and cold weather activities. Hot weather presents another dimension to the dehydration equation and should be monitored carefully. At some point, extreme heat will warrant a cool place to stop and get out of the sun. The normal body temperature for the German Shepherd is between 100 and 102°F (38–39°C). The easiest way to think about this is remembering that his temperature is slightly higher than our own, so he can withstand slightly lower temperatures than we can and not quite as high a temperature. He should never be left outside, exposed to either extreme heat or cold. If you are affected by the temperature, he probably is too.

Poisoning

For some kinds of poisoning, you will want to induce vomiting, whereas for others you will not. It is good to know the difference before the emergency occurs.

Topical exposure Rinse with clear water, followed by bathing the area with a mild soap and water.

Ingestion (corrosive and petroleum-based substances) Administer charcoal orally and get medical help immediately.

Ingestion (other nonpetroleum poisons) Induce vomiting (conscious animals only) and get medical help immediately. One teaspoon of hydrogen peroxide for each ten pounds of body weight can quickly induce vomiting.

Some poisons have antidotes:

- Ethylene glycol
- Acetaminophen
- Organophosphates
- Permethrins
- Lead
- Anticoagulant rodenticides
- Metaldehyde
- Snake venom
- Zinc
- Arsenic

You might want to keep a desktop icon on your computer for the ASPCA Poison Control Center: *www.aspca.org/pet-care/poison-control/*.

Poisonous snakes, spiders or other poisonous creatures Give an antihistamine immediately, such as Benadryl, and get your dog to your veterinarian immediately. These poisons work by swelling the tissue around the entry point and in the respiratory tract. Giving an antihistamine immediately in a large enough dose can help until medical help is present.

Bleeding

If your German Shepherd is cut and bleeding, the primary issue is to stop the bleeding. Cover with a gauze pad or other sterile cloth and apply pressure. Then seek emergency treatment as soon as possible. This common procedure is just the same as with human first aid. When the bleeding subsides, get the appropriate treatment, depending on the severity of the wound. Like children, your dog will run and play and scrape his body up. Which scrapes require further treatment is something you will have to decide. Just remember that he is subject to infection just as you are.

Seizures

There are more than 100 causes of seizures in the canine species. Of those, more than 90 percent are caused by what is called idiopathic epilepsy. Idiopathic epilepsy simply means the cause is unknown (*idio*—Greek for "to not know") (*pathic*—"the cause"). This disease is more common in some

CAUTION

Vigorous exercise is a delight to your German Shepherd, but it is also a time when injuries can happen. It is good to check out an area before you go and turn him loose in the wild. Check for rocky ground and stickers that can hurt his feet, cliffs and drop-offs that can be a hazard, and other features of the terrain. Also be careful of trails that are open to motorized off-road vehicles. Dogs on the trail and motorized vehicles can be a prescription for disaster.

breeds than others and is found in the German Shepherd. It is believed to be genetic, and reputable breeders will not breed an epileptic dog. The result is that this disease, though still present in the breed, occurs less frequently than it did in days gone by. It is believed to affect fewer than 2 percent of German Shepherds.

Although idiopathic epilepsy is the major cause of seizures, there are many other causes as well. If your dog suffers from a seizure, you will want to check for poisoning or an elevated body temperature, since most seizures are triggered in the brain and are neurological in origin. In any event, get medical help as soon as possible. The old treatment during a seizure was to place something in the dog's mouth to keep him from biting his tongue, but objects can easily move into the throat and choke him. It is better to just stay with him, making sure he does not move into other dangers, and allow the seizure to move to a conclusion and the resolution phase. If the seizure does not subside in three to ten minutes, emergency treatment is warranted.

The best first aid you can practice is preventive. Search through your house and yard for things your dog can get into, assume that he will if it is available, and then eliminate the risk. Also keep your veterinarian's phone number close to the phone and available when needed. If there is an emergency animal clinic in your town, you might also want to keep that number readily available for afterhours emergencies.

(See also First Aid Kit on page 79.)

Shock

Shock is caused by a lack of effective circulation. It is a life-threatening condition that is reversible if treated in time. Causes of shock include severe loss of blood, burns, trauma, snakebites, poison, lack of oxygen, prolonged vomiting, prolonged diarrhea, and others.

Symptoms to look for:

- Pale color in gums/inside eyelids; capillary refill time greater than two seconds
- Dry lips and gums, dehydration
- Excessive drooling in some poison cases
- Weak femoral pulse, rapid 150 to 200 beats per minute
- Rapid heart rate
- Cool extremities
- Hyperventilation, rapid breathing generally over 25 breaths per minute
- Confusion, restless, anxiousness
- General weakness
- Advanced stages of shock:
- Continued depression and weakness to the point of not being able to move or becoming unresponsive or unconscious
- Dilated pupils
- Capillary refill time greater than four seconds
- White mucous membranes
- Body temperature below 98°F (37°C), taken rectally

Treatment

- Ensure adequate ventilation.
- Control any bleeding.
- Keep dog quiet and calm to prevent further injury.
- Keep body temperature normal.
- Get dog to veterinarian so fluid replacement and medication can be started.

An injured dog or an animal in shock may not recognize you. Your own dog may bite you out of pain or fear. It is very important to talk to the dog in very soft and reassuring tones. If the dog is having trouble breathing or panting heavily, do not put a muzzle on him. If you do place a muzzle on the dog, you must monitor him at all times and remove it at the first sign of overheating or vomiting. Get help, if possible, from someone who can help hold the dog, so you can do an examination and/or treat the dog.

German Shepherd Nutrition

A few German Shepherds are picky eaters. A few are ravenous eaters, devouring anything and everything. Most are good eaters but are not inclined to make eating their sole life's goal. All German Shepherds love a good treat and a reassuring hug. They are motivated to please and will do most anything with the reinforcement of the treat and some praise.

Feeding has been made easier with the advancement of nutrition in our generation. Many premium products exist to deal with the specific needs of the German Shepherd. There are even breed-specific kibbles available today that may be more expensive but whose value may be worth it to you. There are websites that compare dog foods for nutritional content and rate them according to the value of the content versus the price they charge.

By and large, it is a good idea to avoid those pet foods that are made to appeal to the "price only buyer." The cheapest may not be the most economical if it does not provide for the health and comfort of your dog. Most premium foods are adequate and come in a variety of applications: puppy food, adult food, and maintenance diet for older dogs.

Puppy food usually contains higher amounts of protein than adult food, but some breeders contend that too much protein can be too rich for the German Shepherd. Certain puppy maladies such as panosteoitis can be treated by reducing the amount of protein in the diet. Check with your veterinarian, who may recommend the brand that they sell at a higher price, and then compare ingredients and price. Saving money is always good unless it does not provide the proper nutrition for your dog.

The final guide is, Does he like it, does he eat it, and does his coat and stool look like he is getting what he needs? Yes, check his stool. You can learn a lot by checking what comes out of him. Your breeder or veterinarian can help you learn what to look for. The color will be different, depending on the food you feed, but it should be firm but not hard, consistent in color and texture, and not contain larvae or blood. Black stool may indicate blood from the upper intestinal tract and fresh red blood may indicate blood from the lower digestive tract or bowel. In either event, this is a serious emergency and should be attended to immediately.

Kibble, Canned, or Other Forms

Kibble starts out in a wet form, but is then dried and put into bags. It can last long enough not to spoil before it is consumed, but care should be taken in damper climates. Kibble is formulated to contain all the necessary nutrients that dogs need, but may not be as appealing to some dogs as the damp canned foods. An ideal solution is to make the kibble the main nutrient source and then to put canned food with it to make it appealing and more tasty. This can also be accomplished with home-prepared ingredients such as hamburger, chicken, or whatever meat you think your dog might like. He does have taste buds and will enjoy a degree of variety in his diet.

Some people choose to make their own dog food from scratch, mixing beef, rice, oatmeal, yogurt, and other ingredients. One major kennel on the West Coast has been doing this for years with good results. Most people prefer the convenience of commercially prepared foods, knowing that professionals have consulted on the ingredients that are necessary for good health.

There is a great degree of controversy over the best food for dogs and the best form of the food. Given the longevity of the modern domesticated dog it appears that whichever "food camp" you land in, your dog will be better off than his ancestors. It is a good idea to proceed with caution when deciding on a diet and to stay with it once you have decided. The digestive tract of the canine is easily upset by any diet changes. There are also a variety of supplements on the market for dogs that make various claims from sane to impossible. Check with your veterinarian before deciding on a supplement. As a general rule, although some supplements have beneficial ingredients, most are unnecessary given the research that goes into the major dog foods.

Check the ingredients label to see what's in there. Certain grains, like corn, are not highly digestible in dogs. Dogs are primarily carnivores and should get the majority of their nutrition from meat. The German Shepherd can be overloaded with too much protein and too little balance in his diet, so choose carefully.

Monitoring Your German Shepherd's Weight

As in humans, dogs' body styles come in all sizes and shapes. But in the purebred dog you should expect more consistency in structure and style. The German Shepherd is a medium-sized dog, and his weight should be proportional to his frame. Most people overfeed their dogs and the dogs carry too much weight around and enjoy too little exercise. Keeping that in mind can help in limiting his intake and keeping him able to do the work for which he is designed. Although he may beg for more and eat far more than he needs, he will be happier and healthier if he is at working weight and able to move freely and easily. The German Shepherd lives to move, to run, to play, and to work. Extra pounds will limit both his usefulness and his enjoyment of his working nature. Puppies, in particular, should not be allowed to become too heavy. Some structural problems are increased by excess weight.

FYI: Dog Food Comparisons

There are a number of Internet sites that compare dog food content, nutritional value, and even price. Although some are from manufacturers touting their product, others are created by breeders or interested people who simply want to share their findings. Here are a few of the many available:

www.best-dog-food-guide.com/aafco.html

www.peteducation.com/article.cfm?c=2+1661&aid=662

www.consumersearch.com/dog-food

www.dogfoodanalysis.com

www.doberdogs.com/menu.html

dogfoodchat.com/dog-food-ratings/

www.gooddogmagazine.com/drydogfood.htm

www.dogfoodscoop.com/dog-food-comparison.html

Note: The above is not a complete list and is for informational purposes only. The author and publisher do not have any interest in these sites, nor do we recommend them or agree or disagree with the information in them.

Dog food sites can be informational but can also be biased, depending on the owners of the site. While providing useful information, some have a hidden or not so hidden agenda, like their own product or a particular kind of diet.

The German Shepherd is a single-tracking gaiting dog. That is, when gaiting, the front feet and the rear feet on both sides, although moving at different times, should come down on a relatively straight line toward the center of the dog. He will move more like a bicycle with a single track than a car with two tracks. This is more efficient in herding, because he can turn easily from side to side while leaning into the turn. If the dog becomes too massive, he will lack this agility and mobility, and the bulk between the front legs or rear legs will keep him from this single-track gait.

Of course, keeping his weight under control will help him be more active and able to do whatever job you have given him. Like people, too much weight is bad for the heart and the body in general. The preferred way to manage his weight for most breeders is to feed measured amounts twice a day. Free feeding, the practice of leaving food available all the time, is not recommended.

Feeding Raw

There is a movement in our day to "go back to nature" in feeding. The general philosophy is that the dog was once a wild animal that was domesticated and is now being fed dog food that is inadequate for his needs. Others believe that the domestic dog is the animal from which wild dogs sprang. Whichever perspective on their origin is accurate we may never know. That is, few people alive today predate the dinosaurs, although opinions to the contrary do surface from time to time.

What medical science does give us is some facts that need to be considered when making that leap from commercially prepared food to raw diets. There are risks involved and diseases that come through raw meat and meat that is improperly prepared. Here are some of the diseases that can be encountered:

- **Bacillus anthracis** Occasionally occurs in North America
- **Burkholderia (Pseudomonas) pseudomallei** May be present in meat from horses with glanders.
- **Campylobader spp.** Frequent cause of human enteric infection in the United States; Household contact with dogs is significant risk factor for humans for campylobacteriosis; Common contaminant of raw poultry
- **Clostridium botulinum** C. botulinum toxin may occur in bacon and harm dogs if not destroyed by cooking
- **Clostridium perfringens** Common cause of enteritis in dogs
- **Diphyllobothrium latum, Opisthorchis tenuicollis, Dioctophyme renale, and Nanophyetus salmincola (the vector of Neorickettsia helminthoeca)** Food-borne parasites in raw fish
- **Echinococcus multilocularis, and £ granulosus** Transmissible from dogs to humans, cattle, swine, and sheep
- **E. coli 0157:H7** Identified in dog feces; Documented to cause illness in greyhounds fed raw meat
- **Francisella tularensis** Endemic in rabbits, muskrats, and beavers
- **Listeria monocytogenes** Reported to cause abortion in dogs
- **Mycobacterium bow's and M. tuberculosis** From organ meat in infected livestock and in wildlife reservoirs
- **Neospora caninum** Dogs eating infected tissues (aborted fetuses and placentas) can become ill and shed oocysts in feces, passing infection to cattle.
- **Pseudorabies (Aujeszky's disease)** Documented in dogs fed lungs from infected pigs
- **Rabies** Potential public health risk
- **Salmonella spp.** Frequent contaminants in raw meat; Salmonella-related gastroenteritis outbreaks in dogs fed raw meat are well documented; Zoonotic potential if proper hygienic practices are ignored; Dogs may become subclinical carriers
- **Sarcocystis spp.** Dogs eating infected meat may excrete sporocysts into the environment and present hazard for livestock.
- **Staphylococcus aureus and Bacillus cereus** May produce toxin in moist food that incubates before feeding; Taenia hydatigena and T. ovis; Causes lesions in livestock that result in tissue condemnation at slaughter; dogs ingesting these tissues contaminate environment with eggs infectious to livestock.

- **Toxacara canis and Baylisascaris procyonis** Infected dogs may shed infective eggs into the environment and transmit disease to other dogs or humans, where it can cause visceral larval migrans.
- **Toxoplasma gondii** From swine; can infect dogs
- **Trichinella spiralis** From undercooked pork, walrus, seal, and bear meat
- **Yersinia enterocolitica** Contaminates as much as 89 percent of commercially available raw meat; Household transmission from dogs to people can occur.

(Adapted from LeJeune JT and Hancock DD. "Public health concerns associated with feeding raw-meat diets to dogs." JAVMA. 2001; 219(9): 1222–1225.)

Of course, there are risks involved in the handling contamination of prepared foods also and recalls that periodically underscore the lack of care by some manufacturers or the inclusion of ingredients into prepared foods that are dangerous. There seems to be no absolutely safe regimen that can eliminate all risk.

Whatever decision you make in providing the best diet for your German Shepherd, just be sure that you have as many facts as you can find and that you are prepared for the result. If in doubt, consult with your veterinarian on what he recommends before changing his diet.

Mistaken Ideas About Feeding

1. Dogs should fast once a week.

There are no medical findings that this carryover from a human practice has any health value to dogs.

2. The fasting dog works better.

Although a heavy meal before vigorous activity may make us or our German Shepherd lethargic, there is some evidence that a light meal a couple of hours before vigorous activity can support the caloric demands of the activity.

3. Our pets should eat what we eat.

Dogs are primarily carnivores, whereas humans are omnivorous. Our dietary needs are quite different and our gastrointestinal tract works differently. There are few corollaries between the two bodily systems.

4. Dogs need variety in their diet.

Although our pets may enjoy the treat of different flavors, they are far more apt to be satisfied with the same food at each meal than we are. Consistency in their main food source can aid in consistency in the digestive process and in the lessening of gastrointestinal upsets.

5. Dogs should be fed only once a day.

Most dogs can adapt to a once-a-day feeding plan or whatever frequency we provide for them, but studies have shown that some intestinal problems are less frequent with a twice-a-day feeding schedule. Notably among those studies is one on bloat/torsion. A twice-a-day feeding schedule seems to have more benefits than drawbacks.

Exercise

Exercise is a vital part of the health of the German Shepherd. He lives to move and to work. He loves it and he needs it. He should be in shape to do the work he is trained to do and to do it for extended periods. Although it is not good to start the young dog off on an exhaustive regimen of hard exercise, it is a good idea to provide him with enough exercise to make his muscles and cardiovascular system work well. The standard calls for a dog that is well muscled. The entire concept of the German Shepherd is of a dog able to work.

Although you may not be able to keep pace with him in his exercise needs, you might find some creative ways to allow him to exercise with you and also without you. Setting up a run that is long and narrow for this purpose and finding a motivator to keep him moving up and down that run for more lengthy periods of time is a good idea. Breaking his exercise into segments and letting each member of the household take a segment will also facilitate a good exercise program. However you do it, it is good to allow him the time and joy of plenty of exercise. You will both enjoy it and benefit from it.

Although road working using a bicycle is common, you should use some caution if you are thinking about using a motorized vehicle like an ATV or car in training. This may seem convenient for you, but it can be very danger-ous for your German Shepherd. Some of the tragedies of injured dogs who have been hit by a car or motorcycle in training involve dogs that have been cautious for months or years. One lapse of judgment or errant movement toward something of interest has resulted in serious injury or death. Besides, you may need the exercise as badly as he does.

Chapter Seven

Training and Activities

One of the great parts of your experience with your German Shepherd will be in training. He will learn easily and want more. He will delight in his training time and be thrilled when he pleases you. He will learn fast and retain it for his lifetime. Although retraining will reinforce the training, you can expect him to be an obedient dog for your entire life together.

If you choose to go to a training class, expect to be bored but proud as you have to wait for the rest of the class to catch up to what your German Shepherd learned easily the first time. You can also be proud when the instructor makes you the example of those who have been working really hard to learn the lessons, when you know you didn't work very hard at all. Your dog was just smarter than the rest and more willing to please.

Basic Training

Most communities have an assortment of training classes available. The value of a class is that your dog will be in a social environment, working with other dogs of various kinds and sizes. This social environment is a great way to develop temperament and to set social guidelines. Being with people and other animals is an essential part of training him to be a good citizen both at home and in the community.

Finding the right training class can be difficult if you have many from which to choose. Some of the larger pet store chains offer classes as a service to their customers and as a way of attracting retail traffic. Most have standards that they set for their trainers and classes for their trainers. These can be a valuable asset.

Many cities and counties offer training classes through their recreation department or animal-control department. The trainers for these are often people in the community who have surfaced as experts in their field and who can give competent instructions in a group setting.

Dog clubs and dog training clubs exist in many larger communities and may offer classes. Some are breed specific so that your German Shepherd will be with others of his own kind. Some clubs offer both basic and advanced training, leading to obedience competition and titles, whereas most of the other classes are for purely recreational purposes and designed to make the average pet a better and more obedient companion. You will have to decide what is best for you and how far you want to take the training.

Every dog, particularly the German Shepherd, should have a basic obedience class. This is because your German Shepherd is smart enough to enjoy the training and also smart enough to get into mischief without it. He needs a job to enjoy and a person with whom to enjoy it. He needs the challenge and the joy of meeting and exceeding the challenge. He is competitive by nature and will love the process of learning and gaining recognition for his accomplishments.

Finding the Right Trainer

There still remain some of the heavy-handed training methods of the past. Although they may have been effective in achieving the desired result, they have been largely proven unnecessary. Few German Shepherds need heavy-handed training. He is by nature smart, curious, and desiring to please, so all he will need is a disciplined program of training and lots of praise.

Probably the easiest method of selecting a trainer is to interview a few. Check to see that they have sufficient training themselves and that they have enough experience doing it to be trustworthy. Then attend a class or two of the ones you think might be best beforehand to see if you can work well with the trainer and in the setting.

Training Steps

The basic training commands are *sit*, *down*, *stay*, *come*, and *heel*. Each is an essential part of exercising control over your dog.

Sit

To teach him to sit, simply use a treat and offer it to him, then move the treat over his nose and backward until he sits to get it. When he does sit, say "*Sit*," give him the treat, and give him praise.

FYI: Training Sounds

Many dog sports require an interactive response between dog and owner or handler. "Putting them on the sound" involves the use of a handheld clicker, a whistle, horn, bell, or other noisemaking item. The German Shepherd is easily trained to his one particular sound.

The process of clicker, bell, or whistle training is to use the sound-making item when you call him to dinner or when out walking to tell him to come and then produce the sound. You can also make the sound and then reward him with a treat as reinforcement. In no time he will associate the sound with the command and respond to the sound without the command.

This is particularly important when you want him to know your location when you are out of sight or when there are other dogs in the sport and you want him to respond to you alone. He will learn his sound out of all the others present and know that it comes from you.

It does no good to tell him to sit if he doesn't know what that means, so the act of sitting is the starting point. When he sits, say "*Sit*." He will learn to associate his action with your word in short order. Some trainers will have you stand at their side and push on their rear when you say "*Sit*," but most will have you work from a standing position in front of him and just move the treat over his head so that his expected response is to set back in order to get the treat. With the German Shepherd you will be surprised at how easily he understands and responds.

Be sure to reinforce each obedient response with praise. This positive reinforcement will lift his spirits and make him want to comply. Like a child, he will rise to the level of your expectation and find personal satisfaction in pleasing you. After he learns what *sit* means, put him on lead and work from his right side (dog on your left) and give him the command while gently lifting the lead a little. When he does this a few times, give him lots of praise. He is now sit trained.

Down

The *down* command starts with the dog in the sitting position. From there the treat can be offered toward the nose but lowered to the ground so that he has to go down to get it. As this process is repeated and the *down* position is learned, you will want to also use the word *down* and use the opened hand, palm toward the dog, then moved downward until it is flat or parallel with the floor and lowered toward the floor. As he learns to go down, he will also learn the associated hand signal.

Some dogs are particularly resistant to the down action. For them, you can work on lead. Simply let out enough slack in the lead that it is touching the floor, and then step onto it with one foot with the lead looped underneath the foot. Then repeat the command and offer the treat downward to the floor

Helpful Hints

An easy treat for training can be made by cutting a hot dog into small slices and then putting it in the microwave for a couple of minutes.

This will dry out the hot dog and make it somewhat hard, and it can then be carried in a bag in your coat pocket. After each command and response, give a lot of praise and a slice of hot dog.

Boiled liver also works well after being microwaved, but some dogs do not tolerate liver as well. Too much liver or any kind of treat is not a good thing, so rely primarily on praise.

Note: DO NOT return your coat to the closet for three months with forgotten treats in the pocket. Not a good idea at all!

while lifting the lead and allowing it to slip under your foot, pulling him gently downward. He will have no option but to follow the lead and thus get the point of what *down* means. After repeating this several times, you should be able to do the exercise without the lead and he should respond accordingly.

Stay

Stay will take a little longer, but hang in there; he will get it before long. Usually the first part of the training is the most important and will take the longest. Put him on lead and work from the side (always the same side). Have him sit, then place your hand in front of him, palm toward him, say *"stay"* and take a step or two forward. It is expected that he will want to follow you and will move from his sitting position. Don't scold him; just repeat the *sit* command and start over. He will soon understand that this new command, *stay*, means to not move. As he obeys the *stay* command, be sure to give him the treat, but rather than allowing him to come to you to get it, move back to his position and give it to him while he is down. This reinforces his position in relationship to the command rather than confusing him by rewarding him for coming to the treat.

Combining the *sit* command with the *stay* command and the *down* command with the *stay* command is the next step. Practice this until he obviously gets the point and is working with the combined commands together, then increase your distance from him. As you move farther and farther away and he remains in his position, you establish control without your immediate presence. The objective of this exercise is to be able put him on *down/stay* and go into a building and find him waiting in the same position when you return.

Come

Come is the recall command that ends the stay and releases him to come to you. This one is relatively easy to learn because he wants to be at your side anyway. As you move farther and farther away in your *stay* training, you will want to end each training event with your returning to him or having him come to you.

After learning this basic exercise, you may want to increase the degree of difficulty by having him come to you and then having him stop and sit or lie down in the middle of his return. To do so, use your hand signals along with your voice command and tell him to *"Stay," "Sit,"* or *"Down"* as you desire.

These four commands, *sit, down, stay,* and *come,* form the basis of all obedience commands and most of the sports that you may want to pursue in the future.

Heel

Heel is the command for having your dog walk with you on your left side and slightly behind, so that the head is at your side and the body is trailing behind. This position is used in protection work so that the dog is ready for any eventuality, but the right hand of the handler is available for use with a side arm. In the obedience ring, this is the position from which all the exercises stem.

This is also a good position of control when you are out walking him and need to avoid other people walking dogs or simply keeping him from chasing a cat or other animal and getting into the street or other dangerous place.

Breed Truths

The German Shepherd is one of the most easily trained and most obedient of all breeds—when you are present.

Expect to find things missing off the counter, end tables, or other places if he is left alone. Although his behavior is modified in training, he will still have a mind of his own, and his curiosity and appetite will often get the better of his training. So prepare for it when you leave and be sure to keep anything dangerous or poisonous out of range.

His mischievousness and playfulness will be both delightful and at times frustrating. Enjoy them and learn to laugh a lot!

The training steps are simple. Put him on lead and walk with him, snapping the lead slightly as he either lags behind or pulls out ahead, and say *"heel."* In short order he should understand the desired position at your side and comply. The exception to this training would be conformation dogs, which typically are trained to run in front of the handler. They should not heel or should do some advanced training to know the difference between *heel* and *go*.

Each of these steps should be reinforced with much praise. The entire training session should not be too long. Keeping the training within your dog's attention span is important so that he does not lose interest and become bored. The length of time can vary as he gains competence, but for the puppy with no training, 15 to 20 minutes is adequate. This time should expand as he grows older and he moves forward in his training. If you are in a training class that lasts for an hour and your puppy loses interest, it might be well to explain to the instructor that you would like to be excused when this happens. It is better to have more training classes of shorter duration than fewer, longer ones. You want this to be a fun time where his interest is piqued and his energy level is high. Be careful that it does not become a negative time where he is worn out, given negative feedback about himself, or overwhelmed by the class content.

As a general rule, take the steps easily, and sequentially, and practice for short durations frequently.

There are other commands that you may want to use that are less formal but good rules for around the house and yard. *Leave it* is a common command to get dogs' attention and keep them from picking up something that is offensive or dangerous to them. The profoundly simple word *no* also conveys your displeasure with an activity or direction. *Be nice* can also reinforce his need to get along with other pets or people.

Training Tests

The obedience trial will give you a view of how good the training is. Before you enter, you might want to visit a show that has obedience competition to see what is involved. Then, if you are so inclined, join the obedience club and start the exacting training that will allow you to compete at the show level. The levels of competition are as follows:

NOVICE Class—Beginners
Heel on Leash and Figure Eight
Heel Free
Stand for Examination
Recall Long Sit (1 minute)
Long Down (3 minutes)

OPEN Class—Second Level
Heel Free and Figure Eight
off leash
Drop on Recall, Retrieve on Flat
Retrieve Over High Jump
Broad Jump
Long Sit (3 minutes)
Long Down (5 minutes).

UTILITY—The Third and Highest
Level
Signal Exercise
Scent-Directed Retrieve
Moving Stand and Examination
Directed Jumping
Other tests can also help to demonstrate the level of training your German Shepherd has. One of the more popular is the German Shepherd Dog Club of America's Temperament Test. In this test, your dog will be asked to experience a variety of settings and the evaluator will grade the responses for a final score. The settings are as follows:

CAUTION

When looking for a puppy training class, be cautious about where you go. Not all trainers use methods that are good for the German Shepherd.

Some classes are poorly supervised, with dogs going in all directions, and you might find your German Shepherd objecting to his space being violated. It is good to have him with other dogs for training, but you will not want people bringing their dogs up to him without him giving them permission. He will have more definite territorial definition than other breeds. He will also be at the head of the class, learning far more easily than the rest. He will also benefit from a soft-touch method without harsh treatment.

Positive reinforcement will work best for him.

1. Behavior Toward Strangers: objective to measure the dog's reaction to strangers in a nonthreatening situation.
   – Neutral Stranger
   – Friendly Stranger
2. Reaction to Aural Stimuli (Noise): objective to measure alertness to aural stimuli and the degree of investigative behavior toward the stimuli.
   – Can-Rattling
   – Gun Test
3. Reaction to Visual Stimuli: objective to measure the dog's reaction to sudden visual stimuli, degree of investigative behavior, and startle recovery.
   – Umbrella

4. Footing Test: objective to measure the dog's reaction to unusual footing.
   – Footing Test
5. Aggressive Stranger: objective to measure the dog's capacity to recognize and react in a positive, guarding manner to a potentially threatening situation and, in the event of a threat, to react in an aggressive, confident manner.

You will find these and many other training exercises and tests to be a fun and rewarding way to keep your training advancing and sharp. You may also want to check out the American Kennel Club's Canine Good Citizen Certificate program at *http://www.akc.org/events/cgc/program.cfm*.

Activities for the German Shepherd

Of all the breeds, the German Shepherd is the most versatile, with the ability to do far more than the owner can possibly have time for. He can work in a variety of jobs, compete in a variety of sports, and serve as a therapy dog in between activities.

Usually it is the owner who chooses the activities. He is capable of many, but the interest of you the owner will determine which he will pursue. Probably he will not care, as long as you are doing something together.

Agility
One of the sports growing in popularity is agility. Agility is a high-energy race through a course of jumps, tunnels, rings, through or over obstacles, and through weaves. It is a timed event and is graded for the size of the dog.

Dogs love it and have great fun conquering the course and working with their owner. Several competitions have made it onto TV, but if you have never seen one, go to the AKC website and look up one in your area and take your dog.

AKC agility events are for registered dogs at least six months old. Titles are awarded and more; the dogs consider it their Disneyland. He will love it.

Agility clubs have sprung up in many communities, and the sport is offered by AKC-affiliate clubs and other registries.

Schutzhund

Schutzhund originated in Germany as a means of evaluating the overall working ability of a German Shepherd. It involves three phases: Tracking, Protection, and Obedience. This sport is intense and requires hours of training. It involves competitive events where the entered dogs are judged on each of the phases and receive a rating at the end. Not all dogs have the temperament for this sport, and they should be tested by a competent trainer before beginning the training. Training happens best at an early age for this sport.

Schutzhund clubs are among the fastest-growing sports with the German Shepherd and are worth investigating. They are a delight to watch, and who knows, you might find that both you and he are a good fit for this energetic and competitive sport.

Schutzhund trials and training are offered by the German Shepherd Dog Club of America—Working Dog Association (GSDCA–WDA), Deutscher Verband der Gebrauchshundsportvereine America (DVGA), and United Schutzhund Club of America (UScA). These clubs also offer breeder referrals to people who are interested in a puppy for their sport.

Tracking

Tracking is a competition of its own, but is also used by local search-and-rescue clubs as a resource to law enforcement and disaster agencies. Local SAR (search-and-rescue) clubs provide training, and the German Shepherd Dog Club of America has a division—the Working Dog Association—that provides training for schutzhund trials, which involves tracking. Many communities have search-and-rescue associations that have tracking training and trials. An Internet search will reveal many search-and-rescue clubs in various communities. Some are national organizations with local chapters.

Dogs with tracking skills may specialize in cadavers, drug detection, insect-sniffing, cancer detection, and a variety of other specialties in which the training singles out one specific item for the dog to detect. This can be a great activity for competition and recreation, and a useful service to the community.

Therapy Dog Work

The German Shepherd can be of great value as a therapy dog. His sensitive nature and his ability to adjust his activities to a given environment work well in a therapeutic setting. German Shepherds have been used in hospitals, convalescent homes, with Alzheimer's patients, in children's wards, and beyond. Studies have shown that the presence of a dog has a calming effect on patients and may even be a tool for reducing pain. The Alpha Society Inc. and Therapy Dogs International are among many organizations that invite membership in a national network of therapy dogs. Most of these agencies require that the candidate pass the AKC Canine Good Citizen Test or a similar test from a registering or training club. The German Shepherd Dog Club's Temperament Test has been accepted by many of these agencies.

A therapy dog is not a service dog and is not covered by the American Disabilities Act, so they do not have a guaranteed right to access anywhere. Access to a hospital, treatment center, or other place where they might work has to be by the organization itself. Many organizations provide training and certification for therapy dogs, including St John Ambulance, the Alpha Society (Tampa, FL), Delta Society (Bellevue, WA), and TDInc (Cheyenne, WY).

Hunting

Believe it or not, the German Shepherd has been successfully used as a hunting dog. He has been used for bird hunting and large-animal hunting because of his keen scenting ability and his work ethic. So if you are a hunter, go ahead and do the training and you will find him adaptive to what you are doing. Be prepared, however, if you hunt birds. When you arrive at the hunting dog training class, the owners of the bird dogs will laugh, at least until you start hunting. Most bird dogs are "soft mouth dogs," meaning they by nature do not injure the bird, holding it gently. The German Shepherd will probably not excel in bird dog competition, but they have been used for this purpose.

Conformation Training

There is little you can do to train for the conformation show. The conformation dog is one that meets the standard more closely than others in the breed. The activity involves moving around the ring so the judge can evaluate movement and stand for examination so the judge can feel the structure of the dog. You can train him to move out in front of the handler and to remain still for examination, but in terms of training him to win, you cannot. Judges will make the decision on what they see alone. If you are interested in this sport, a good first step is to find a breeder or club that is involved and have your dog evaluated. One evaluation may not give a true picture, for judges

ACTIVITIES Junior Showmanship

If you have children in the home and are considering conformation as an activity, you might want to consider getting involved with Junior Showmanship. This activity involves children 9–18 years old in competition with other children in their age group. The competition is not related to judging the dog but in judging the abilities of the Junior Handler. This sport teaches good sportsmanship and the art of showing and handling the German Shepherd in the ring.

As a stepping-stone to this competition, many children start in 4-H Clubs that hold dog shows, including mixed-breed dogs, focused on the handling rather than the dog.

Check out these websites for further information:

* *www.akc.org/kids_juniors/*
* *gsdca.org/gsdca_joomla/index.php/events/junior-handling*
* *4-h.org/*

see different things and not all evaluations are the same. But if after three or four evaluations all agree that he is not a conformation dog, showing him may be frustrating to both him and you. There are a variety of registries and clubs that sponsor conformation shows, including the American Kennel Club, the German Shepherd Dog Club of America, the United Kennel Club, the White German Shepherd Dog Club, the Canadian Kennel Club, and the National Kennel Club. More are listed on the Internet.

Herding

One of the more fun things to do with the German Shepherd is the basic task for which the breed was developed—herding. A herding test will help to determine if your dog has the instinct for herding. A few will be too strong and want lamb chops rather than herd the flock, but most will have an innate ability for the herding task. The evaluator will be able to guide you toward training and to the competitions that are held in this sport. Most regional member clubs of the German Shepherd Dog Club of America have contacts with herding training and will be glad to include you in their activities.

The Versatile German Shepherd

The German Shepherd breed is adept at so many tasks that it would be impractical to try to do with him all that he is capable of doing. And not every individual dog is capable of everything. If you are interested in a specific job, task, or competition, it would be best for you to involve yourself in that task and then find a dog that excels in it through the contacts you make. If, as with most people, you have already selected the dog and are

now searching for things he will enjoy, it would be well to take him for an evaluation for several things and then make your choice based on how he does in his evaluations.

Trying to force yourself or your dog to do something he is not fond of or is incapable of will produce frustration in you and him. By and large, he can do it all, but as a practical matter, there may be some things he enjoys more and does better.

Not all German Shepherds should be riding around in police cars. Not all should be doing schutzhund trials, and not all should be guide dogs or therapy dogs or what-have-you. Just as with people, German Shepherds differ from each other, and contentment may demand that you find the task he enjoys along with you.

He will enjoy some task that involves physical activity, however, so finding that activity and doing it is important. You might want to explore several before committing to one for which you have the time and energy. He will have both the time and energy if you do. Somewhere around you is a club that has agility equipment or herding activities or other things that both of you will enjoy.

Training for those activities can be as fun as the activities and competition themselves. To see him delight in running through the agility course like a child at a playground is certainly a worthy experience. And the awe of watching his nature released in herding can be nothing short of amazing. To watch the German Shepherd survey the flock and go to work, knowing instinctively what to do, is one of the wonders of the world.

Leash Training

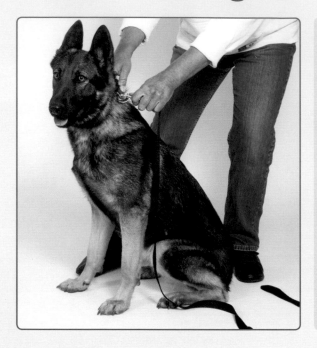

1 Place a collar on the puppy and a leash in the collar and do not pull on the lead. Simply let it trail along where he goes. Lure him along with a treat, walking slightly in front of him. After he has moved forward with you for a minute or so, give him the treat and lots of praise. Then do it again, luring him forward, and giving him the treat after he has moved along several yards.

2 If he strays from your intended path, let him, but lure him back so that the treat is given only after he has followed your directions.

3 If he remains where he is and fusses over the lead, walk a few yards, then move away from him and coax him with the treat.

4 Then pick up the lead and allow him to lead, following him where he wants to go. Finally, exercise control over the direction yourself, rewarding him for following you. Break the training into segments over several short sessions for several days in a row. Leash training for the German Shepherd will not take too long. He will be excited to see the leash and to go for a walk with you in no time.

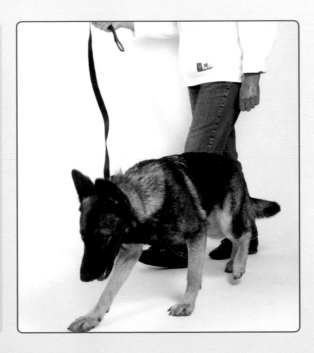

121

The Sit Command

1 Stand in front of him with a treat in hand and move the treat to his nose, then up over the nose to the back of his head, slowly enough for him to respond and follow the direction. This should encourage him to sit back to reach up and get the treat.

2 Keep repeating this movement, giving him the treat each time he sits to get it, while repeating the command, *"Sit."*

3 Then guide him with your hand empty, giving him the treat with the other hand.

4 Finally, use the hand signal for "*sit*" while repeating the exercise until he sits with just the hand signal.

The Stay Command

1 Have him sit on your left side and then say "*stay*," giving him the signal for *stay* with your left hand. If he moves, do not scold, but put him back in the *sit* position and try again. When he does stay for a second or two, praise him and give a treat. Then continue the exercise, adding time to each *stay* segment.

2 When he does this with some competence, tell him to "stay," using your hand signal, and then pivot so that you are in front of him, facing him. Increase the time and reward him for each success.

3 Next, move to a different position, to one side or the other. As you increase the time, walk completely around him, then back to the side or in front and reward him.

4 Keep practicing until you can move clear across a room or a good portion of the yard with him remaining in the *stay* position. Practice for short periods of time and then release him from the session with a cheerful "Okay!" and lots of praise.

Chapter Eight

Grooming the German Shepherd

Visiting a dog show will find the grooming tent or arena a beehive of activity, with Poodles being trimmed, Bichon Frises being powdered, and an infinite variety of breeds being prepared for the show with curlers, ribbons, hoods, scissors, tweezers, and a variety of supplies, instruments, and equipment. Grooming tables will be filled with dogs of various sizes and shapes, being prepared to enter the ring and bring home the prize. The great thing about the German Shepherd is that he is primarily a "wash-and-wear" kind of dog. Even the lofty show German Shepherd requires only a quick bath, a blow dry, and brush-up, and in the ring he goes. While other breeds are being primped and pushed and combed and teased and trimmed, the German Shepherd is wandering through the grooming tent with his master, smiling at the efforts of the more hurried souls who are frantically doing, well, stuff. There are many advantages to having a German Shepherd. Grooming is one of them.

The German Shepherd has a dual coat, consisting of the coarser, longer, and stiffer outer coat and the softer inner coat (undercoat). Molting or shedding will usually occur in the spring and fall seasons but can be affected by the climate or the amount of daylight in your region. Female dogs usually shed just before they come into season.

The outer coat functions primarily as a protector from the elements and contains the majority of his pigment. The inner coat has great insulating value and protects your dog from cold and heat as well. The inner coat is the hair that sheds more readily and may need more help in the process by brushing and loosening.

Grooming Basics

All dogs require grooming, just as with all people, although some people do not understand this basic necessity. The German Shepherd is no different. Even though he requires less grooming than most breeds, he still has some basic requirements that he cannot do for himself. Grooming areas for the German Shepherd are as follows:

- A coat that needs to be cleaned
- A body that needs to be cleaned
- Ears shaped like funnels that work quite well for hearing and for collecting dirt
- Nails that need to be trimmed occasionally
- Teeth that need cleaning
- A regular check of anal sacs, anus, and sexual parts

Bathing

The German Shepherd does not have sweat glands, so he does not need deodorant under the arms. He cools himself by panting and by drinking water, so unlike people, he will not need a daily bath. In fact, some people tend to overbathe their dogs, thinking he needs cleansing as often as we do. The German Shepherd is an active dog and will interact with his outdoor environment easily, so he will need to be cleaned up periodically. How often is largely determined by his activity level, the kind of environment he is kept in, and the kinds of activities in which he engages.

Show dogs are usually bathed before each show for appearance's sake, not necessarily because their health and good grooming demand it. If he is exposed to hiking and hunting and gets wet and muddy, your dog may need to be bathed after each outdoor trip. Along with the bath it is good to inspect him for ticks, fleas, and other visible pests. There are bath preparations that are designed to kill these pests, but some are ineffective and some are toxic to the dog. Be sure to check with your veterinarian for advice on which products are safe.

The bath need not be an ordeal, although the first one is certainly going to be quite an experience. Your dog will learn to love his grooming and will look forward to it. If you bathe indoors, be sure to use water that is warm but not hot. He will tolerate cool water better than water that is too warm. Use a mild shampoo or a commercial dog shampoo. There are many products available that will make him smell great to you but not necessarily to him.

After the bath be sure to dry him off, let him shake, and give him access to run and jump and enjoy the refreshing time of play. Using a dog dryer is ideal. They produce a large volume of air that is warm but not hot and can reduce the drying time from hours to a few minutes. Most dogs learn to love the massaging effect of the high-volume airflow and will twist and turn in delight as they are dried. When he is almost dry, give him a good brushing-out, removing dead hair loosened by the bath. He will feel great and look great.

There are a variety of coat conditioners available that can be applied after the bath. Some are to be rinsed out, whereas others are left in. The key to a good-looking and resilient coat, however, is not in the topical use of conditioners but in the healthy diet.

CHECKLIST

Grooming Supplies

Keep all of your German Shepherd grooming supplies in one place. There are some nice plastic caddies or baskets available that will keep them together and available when you want to find them. You may need to keep this up where he cannot get at it, however, for he will know it is his and might get into it if it is at "dog level."

Here are some items you may want in your grooming kit:

✔ Natural-bristle brush and coat rake
✔ Toothbrush and toothpaste for dogs
✔ Nail trimmer or electric grinding tool
✔ Styptic powder or stick for bleeding nails
✔ Ear solution and cotton balls
✔ Gentle shampoo for dogs
✔ Your flea/tick control medication
✔ Again, make sure to keep this grooming kit out of reach so you can get to it but he can't.

The Daily Once-Over

It is good to do some grooming every day. A good brushing and a check-over is enjoyable to him and can give you good information about how he is doing. Check his coat to see that it is healthy, shiny and not dry and brittle. The coat is a good indicator of the overall health of your German Shepherd.

Check his ears to see if they need cleaning, his toes for any nail damage, and his anal area for any distress. Some German Shepherds are prone to perianal fistulas and impacted anal sacs. The anal sacs are on each side of the anus and can become inflamed if they are not emptied naturally. When they do become inflamed or impacted, they can be emptied by squeezing gently or you can have your veterinarian do this procedure and teach you how.

Perianal fistulas are fissures in the tissue around the anus that can become infected and bleed. An occasional check for anything out of the ordinary will help to find problems early and to reduce the pain he might be going through if those conditions do occur. Impacted anal sacs can be treated, and if they become a serious problem, can be surgically removed.

Perianal fistulas, on the other hand, are a more serious issue. Until recently they were a fatal disease in many cases. They tend to become infected easily and worsen over time. Veterinarians used to treat them surgically, cutting away the infected tissue and sewing them up. The treatment in some cases worked quite well, but in some more extreme cases, the infections ultimately were life threatening. More recently, treatment with cyclosporine has worked wonders to reduce the infection and close the fistula without surgical intervention. Care should be taken, however, to find them early to avoid complications and to reduce the length of treatment for a fistula-prone dog.

Basically your daily grooming is a time to brush, touch, and love your dog and to check him over for any new or developing health problems. Touching all areas of his body can be important to him and to you as well. He cannot examine himself, so that becomes your task. It is not a job to be shunned but enjoyed. Both you and your German Shepherd will learn to enjoy and benefit from this time together.

1. Rub his fur on his back, sides, belly, neck, and legs. Check for any lumps, injuries, or stickers. Burrs and foxtails are particularly problematic if they grow in your environment. Burrs will gather fur around them into a tight ball and can be uncomfortable to him. Foxtails will travel into ears, skin, or the intestinal tract creating serious problems.
2. Look at his eyes. They should be clear without red lines in the white and not clouded. They should look alert and normal.
3. Look at his nose. It should be dry on the outside, and moist on the tip and in the nostril but not runny. It should not have a crusty texture on the top or sides.
4. Check his teeth for any discoloration, black spots, or damage. Dogs can have cavities too. Brush away food particles and scrape off plaque.
5. Shine a light in each ear and check for dirt, redness, or any foreign object. You can also smell the ear. A yeasty, sour smell can be a sign of infection. Clean the ears with an ear cleanser and a cotton swab.
6. Rub the fur and skin around his neck and behind his ears. If you feel a lump, dig down into the fur to see if it is a tick, a growth, or an injury.
7. Look under his tail to see that everything is clean and normal.
8. Pick up each paw and check between the toes for stickers and the pad for injuries. Touch each toe and watch for any pain response.
9. Praise him as you go through the checklist. This is not only a daily checkup but a time of training him to let you have control.
10. If you find anything that is of concern, talk to your veterinarian about it.

Brushing

The purpose of brushing is to release the dead hair from the coat and to remove any dirt and dust that might have accumulated. Brush with the grain of the coat and then brush against the grain, fluffing up the coat and catching those particles that might not be released by brushing with the grain of the coat. When it is shedding time, this regular brushing time will be more important. You will see those clumps of hair that are being shed and can help him get rid of them. It is okay to brush vigorously, but be careful. Some dog's

HOME BASICS
German Shepherd Grooming Schedule

Daily	Weekly	Monthly
Once-over	Trim tips of nails	Bathe/shampoo
Brush coat	Clean ears	Apply pest control
Brush teeth, wash face	Brush teeth if not done daily	

skin is more sensitive than others, and this should always be a positive experience for both you and him.

The kind of brush you use is not as important as the regularity of the process. Some of the metal-studded (pin) brushes are harsher and can hurt if used with too much force. A soft bristle-hair brush is usually just fine. Some pet supply stores have a good variety to choose from, and you may want a soft brush for regular brushing and a coat rake for shedding time.

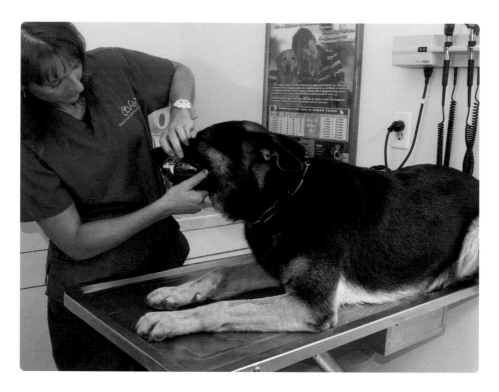

Dental Care

Whether human teeth or dog teeth, they all are subject to a variety of abuse, use, and bacteria. They all need care. There are several methods of tooth care that are used, including giving him something to chew on or brushing his teeth. If you give him bones, be careful that they are not a kind that splinter. One splinter in the digestive tract can be harmful or fatal. A knuckle bone large enough to disintegrate easily or round bones that can be chewed on without being chewed up are the best choices.

Carrots are also a useful tool for cleaning the teeth. He will probably love them, and chewing them up will help to remove the surface tartar from his teeth. But the better instrument for cleaning the teeth is a toothbrush. There are a variety of dog toothpastes, some with liver flavor and others with everything from beef to mint. Try a small tube before investing a lot of money in one to see if he will like it.

Brushing his teeth is similar to brushing our own. Use up-and-down motions to remove food particles and

Helpful Hints

Check his mouth and teeth for splinters after he has chewed a bone of any kind. You may not know if something is lodged in his mouth awkwardly, and if found early, it can be removed without damage.

tartar, brushing both the inside and outside of the teeth. For stubborn accumulations of plaque, a dental scraping tool will work well.

Nail Care

The first time you do his nails, he will be certain that life, as he knows it, is over. Go ahead and clip them anyway. He will get over it and may, like most German Shepherds, not mind it at all in time. There are several types of nail clippers available, but using a human nail clipper is probably going to frustrate you if you try it, because dog nails are shaped differently from human nails. Many people use a Dremel tool or similar grinding device, grinding off the nail tip rather than clipping. Whichever you prefer, the frequency of nail trimming will also depend on the environment in which you live. If you are in the country and he gets

Breed Truths

The German Shepherd's feet are very important to him. He is a hearty dog that loves to move, run, and jump, and, well, act like a dog. His feet are very sensitive and, because of his activities, subject to injury. The hairs between his toes act like "feelers" to increase his sense of touch, as do the nerves in the pads. Check his feet regularly and remove any rocks, mud, sticks, or other objects caught between the toes. Also check for stickers between the toes or in the pads.

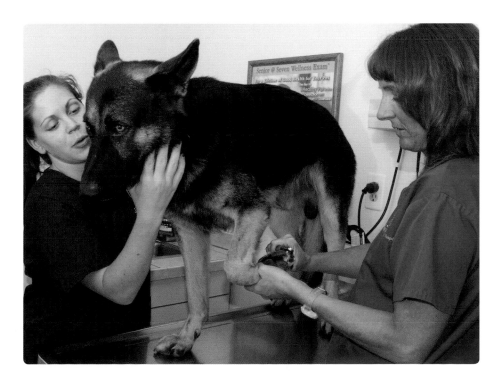

lots of exercise or digs a lot, you may find you need to trim less. But if you are in the city with little place for him to run or dig, the nails might become long sooner.

You will see when the nails are in need of trimming. When they need trimming, or every week, just lay him on his side and clip off the end to square up the nail. Like human nails, his nails have an underlying quick that will bleed if you cut too far. It is a good thing to have a styptic pencil or powder handy in case he does start bleeding. Sometimes it will bleed for a long time, and the styptic powder will help to stop it.

Breed Needs

If your German Shepherd is tilting his head, shaking his head, or rubbing or digging at his ears, get him checked out by your veterinarian. Whereas most dogs have ears that cover the ear passage, German Shepherd ears act like funnels to direct things into the ear. This makes them susceptible to foreign objects and infection.

Ear Care

One of the great and terrible things about the German Shepherd is the shape of his ears. These lovely, attractive, and quite functional appendages are also funnel shaped and will channel objects that fall into the ear on down into the ear canal. Dirt can easily build up, and infection is common without proper ear maintenance.

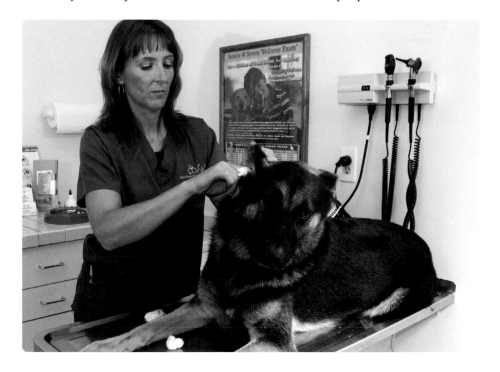

There are a number of ear solutions available, but most of them are a combination of hydrogen peroxide, isopropyl alcohol, and water. Some include boric acid, and some include other preparations. Check with your veterinarian for his or her recommendation.

It is probably a good thing to set a weekly schedule of ear cleaning. Using the ear solution on a cotton ball, clean the visible dirt from the ear, moving it outward away from the ear canal. End the session by squirting a little of the ear solution into the ear and letting your dog shake it out, loosening any debris that is down in the ear. You might want to do this outside.

There are also ear mite treatments available if you live in a humid climate where these pests persist. Most ear mite treatments are designed to dry out the ear to make it an inhospitable environment for the mites.

Just a note about weeds: Foxtails are the great enemy of the German Shepherd. They will move easily down the funnel of the ear and lodge in the inner portion, and can travel from there to the brain. Eliminate foxtails from your yard and watch for the telltale sign of your dog shaking his head and digging at his ear. If it appears that there is something lodged in his ear, get him to your veterinarian as soon as possible. You do not want a foxtail to hurt or kill him.

Pest Control

There are a variety of pests that can invade the German Shepherd world, and he will have no ability to protect himself from them. A variety of internal parasites can hurt or kill him if not treated. One way to manage this is to take a fecal sample to your veterinarian periodically for microscopic inspection. They will be able to identify any parasites or eggs that are of concern. There is also a simple test for heartworms. This parasite can weaken and kill its host if not treated. Again, most of these parasites are regional and tend to be more pervasive in warm, humid climates.

External pests can also be irritating and even fatal if not treated. Ticks carry Lyme disease and other diseases, and fleas can carry a host of animal or human diseases. The best treatment is prevention.

A flea comb used on the underbelly or behind the ears will usually reveal the presence of fleas. To detect ticks, just feel over him, particularly around the neck and behind the ears. When you find one, simply grab it between your thumb and forefinger and pull outward, gently and firmly, until it loses its hold, then dispose of it in alcohol or flush it down the toilet. It is not a bad idea to treat the location of the bite after the tick is removed with hydrogen peroxide or alcohol. If you live in a tick-prone area, ask your veterinarian about a tick collar or a tick-deterrent medication. It is also a good idea to trim grass short and keep your dog out of the tall green grass during the late spring months.

Any flea or tick medication is toxic to the pests so it can kill them. It is designed by the manufacturer to be nontoxic to animals, but there have

CAUTION

Ticks are blood-feeding parasites that most often live in tall grass and weeds. They use the grass to wait for their prey, attaching themselves to any mammal that passes by. A tick attaches itself by inserting its chelicerae (cutting mandibles) and hypostome (feeding tube) into the skin. The hypostome is covered with serrated teeth, which anchor the tick to its host. Physical contact is the method of transportation for ticks. Ticks do not jump or fly, although they can drop or fall onto a host.

been incidents of toxicity, allergic reactions, and even deaths attributed to some preparations. So check with your veterinarian about what is best. They will have health reports of problem medications and pest-control products.

If you prefer not to groom your dog yourself, and want to find a groomer, there are usually many available in most areas of the country. But finding the right one is important. Often, your veterinary clinic will have a groomer renting out part of their facilities and provide some oversight for the safety of their products and services. There are also mobile grooming services available that will come to your house so you can see the process. Just as in selecting a veterinarian, it is perfectly acceptable to ask for references and to check those references. It is also acceptable to ask about the groomer's breed-specific experience. Not everyone who deals with dogs likes or enjoys German Shepherds. Some people, for whatever reason, real or imagined, do not like or trust German Shepherds. While educating them about the German Shepherd may be important, trusting yours to them may not be your best option.

Grooming is an art, and anyone who is in that business should come with some professional training. If you do not know where to start, call your veterinarian or your breeder for suggestions. Often, breeders do grooming as a sideline and will know the essentials for this breed.

Some of the things to look for:

- Level of training
- Has the groomer had professional training and some experience in the trade?
- Kind of equipment
- Are the facilities and equipment safe and sanitary?

Caution: Crate dryers can be particularly dangerous if they are hot and turned on with a dog locked in while the groomer goes about other procedures.

Helpful Hints

- The use of safe supplies
- Are the supplies made for use on dogs and commercially produced?
- What is included?
- Does the grooming include nail clipping, ear cleaning, toothbrushing, etc.?
- How much does it cost? As with all things it is best to find out before you commit.
- How is he housed pending pickup?
- Will he be in a safe, comfortable enclosure while awaiting your return?

Fleas do not just live on dog, cats, or other animals. They nest in the house where their hosts dwell. They are found in carpet and other surfaces that provide them with a place to lay eggs and perpetuate their species. Getting them off the dog is not enough if they have nests in the surrounding environment. If you find an infestation, there are spray insecticides that can help as well as carpet-cleaning solutions that are designed for the task.

If all of that sounds complicated, it may be more so than it needs to be. Although some of us suffer from disabilities that do not permit us to do our own training, grooming, and exercise, for most it is a matter of learning how. Ask your breeder to give you some training or let you observe their grooming procedures. They will usually be more than happy to see you and your German Shepherd and to give you the necessary help in learning how to groom him. It is really not difficult.

Chapter Nine

Senior German Shepherds

Old dogs rule! There is a special place in our hearts for the elderly German Shepherd. Their stately German Shepherd appearance with the touch of gray around the muzzle and the slower pace gives new meaning to the term commanding presence. These are the wise ones who need not fight for position or challenge others for attention. They rule with a glance and control their world by the sheer fact that they are there.

There are telltale signs that a German Shepherd is getting old. The toys are still present, laid carefully at his bedside, but they are seldom tossed or shaken anymore. They have been retired to his private collection of memories. Gray covers his muzzle, and his hearing is noticeably less acute than in his youth. His pace is slower and the weight accumulates far too easily. He has achieved senior status and is now eligible for special notice and special care.

The German Shepherd has a life expectancy of 12 years or less if he has been relatively disease-free. Some have lived to 14 or 15 years, with a few exceptional dogs going beyond that. But 12 years old is an old dog that has exceeded the average. Of course there are no accurate "age of death" statistics simply because, unlike human statistics, no one keeps and publishes those figures.

Various diseases will take many of our beloved dogs long before they reach old age; yet somewhere after eight years of age you will begin to notice the signs of aging. At about this age, it is probably time to visit your veterinarian and start monitoring the aging process. Keeping him healthy will not only prolong his life as much as possible but will also help the quality of his life.

How German Shepherds Age

The aging process in the German Shepherd is much like it is in humans and other animals. Somewhere, hidden from our view and operating without our permission, is a biological clock that ticks relentlessly on, reducing our body from its youthful exuberance to the frailty of old age. The difference is that in the German Shepherd, that clock is set for far fewer years than our own. They simply do not live long enough, and there is nothing we can do to alter that substantially. All we can do is make him as healthy and happy as we can in the few short years he is with us.

Some few German Shepherd owners ignore the prospects of age, and when it comes, they are unable to accept it and deal with it. This is when the elderly regal German Shepherd is passed off to a rescue group or a shelter. This should never be the case.

Planning for old age is wise and will reduce the uncertainty of how to handle it and how to care for him. Though his activity level will change, your dog will still want to be with you, still want to do things with you, still want to do his job, and still want a regular car ride.

If there are drastic changes in him as he grows older, they should not be ignored. Age is a slow and steady continuum, so if there are major sudden changes in his health or demeanor, it is time to get him to the veterinarian for a checkup. Most of the changes you will see are related to the aging of the body; these are slow and steady and are not a matter of medical concern. Things that might be of concern include the following:

- Limping or noticeable pain when walking or running
- A sudden inability to jump on something that had been a regular activity
- Swelling of the lymph nodes in the neck area
- Any bumps or swelling under the skin
- Signs of deafness or blindness, particularly a film growing on the eyes
- Sudden weight loss or gain or refusal to eat his regular meal
- Increased thirst and urination
- Decreased urination or elimination
- Confusion, disorientation, or standing with his head against a wall or in a corner
- Loss of muscle mass, particularly in the rear end
- Dragging the toes of the rear legs, either one or both
- Flinching or yelping when touched in a particular spot
- Uncharacteristic lethargy or a noticeable increase in sleeping
- Rapid eye movement from side to side or up and down
- Loss of balance or apparent dizziness

- Anything that is sudden and out of the ordinary should be a sign that there is trouble to be investigated by a medical professional. All too often people will consult a friend or try to reach a breeder when it is a medical emergency, instead of contacting their veterinarian. Always contact your veterinarian when faced with any of the above conditions.

Changes in Routine

Routine becomes increasingly important as we age, and this is true for the aging German Shepherd. They may enjoy the adventure of a new place to walk or the new friend to meet, but aside from the adventure, he needs his familiar routine. Being a territorial animal, his place is his throne and his observation deck. He will have places where he sleeps, where he eats, and where he waits for those he loves to return to the home. Those places should be kept sacred. You will notice that from an early age, he places himself between you and any approach from outside or into

Helpful Hints

Having a regular yearly checkup with your veterinarian is a good idea throughout the life of your German Shepherd, but as he grows older, it is probably wise to increase the frequency of those visits to every six months or as health issues arise. The sooner you find a problem the easier it is to treat and the less costly.

141

your room. This will continue with age as he guards you with his life.

If you should go through major life changes with an elderly German Shepherd, be sure to include him in the process. If you are moving from one house to another, take him with you to visit the new home and transfer some of his belongings so that he can assume ownership of the new space. When the move is being made, let him participate also. Yes, he will be underfoot and it will take a little more time, but his assimilating the dynamics of the change is as important to him as it is to you. He deserves the honor of inclusion in the changes the family makes.

Other Changes

The Senior Diet At some point you will want to adjust his diet. Weight gain will limit his activity and shorten his life span, so at some point, as you see a couple of pounds added to his body, you might want to shift to a senior maintenance diet. There are many available and probably the brand you are using has a senior food. The reduction of calories and fat will help him to have similar portions and yet not become obese. Check his kidney function as he ages also. If there is a developing kidney problem, your veterinarian may want to reduce his protein intake also.

He may want the same intake and the same frequency of snacks, and it is usually possible to continue those things by altering the content rather than by eliminating them or reducing the portions substantially.

Exercise As your dog ages, he will want to exercise less. That is normal for both dogs and humans, but be sure that, although the exercise level may

taper off, it does not stop. All physical systems in both dogs and humans require exercise. See that he gets an adequate amount of daily exercise, unless there is some physical reason not to, in which case be sure that problem is addressed. If you suspect that he is in pain and may have arthritis or some other joint-disabling problem, be sure to get the proper medication and some reading from your veterinarian about how much exercise is appropriate.

Helpful Hints

As mobility decreases and the exercise regimen is broken by sore joints and stiff muscles, substituting a car ride for the exercise time can be a welcome reward for your German Shepherd. Most place a car ride right up with winning the lottery. While you may have to help him get into and out of the car, he will still enjoy it, and you will be rewarded by seeing his delight.

Although vigorous exercise might have to be tapered off, an easier pace might consume the same amount of time as his younger exercise time but with less speed involved. A long walk at a more leisurely pace can be adequate, and invigorating, and serve to stimulate him and you both physically and emotionally. Keeping his body in shape is the point of physical exercise, but there are other factors that are good for him. All of his senses are involved in exercise. His sense of smell, hearing, and eyesight, and his general need to be outdoors are part and parcel of what the German Shepherd is. He will enjoy every moment of being alive and stimulated in this time of activity with his master.

Grooming The senior's coat may become drier and need extra care. Also, his skin may become thinner and more sensitive, so vigorous brushing may need to give way to a more gentle style. The shedding of hair may be more difficult and he will need your help in removing it. All in all, age takes its toll everywhere, and the extra care necessary for the elderly German Shepherd will pay dividends emotionally for both the dog and owner. Old dogs are simply a delight.

Dogs, like people, need to feel special and appreciated. His regular grooming is part of the communication from you to him that he matters and that his health and good looks are important to you. Grooming is more than a matter of cleanliness. It is also an emotional matter of worth and value. Making the old dog feel important is part of the grooming process.

Serious Health Issues

Genetics being what they are, something will develop in your German Shepherd and will ultimately take his life. No breeding skill will produce an animal that is immune from this life-ending prospect. Each breed of dog has a set of health issues that are more common and that you can watch for as he ages. The German Shepherd is more prone to these problems:

Cancer

Cancer is an increasing phenomenon in many breeds and any nondescript pain or discomfort should be investigated. Cancer is the number one natural cause of death in dogs. Dogs can have different forms of cancer, including bone, skin, breast, connective tissue, oral, and lymphoma cancers.

Probably the greatest risk factor is genetic, but certain environmental factors are suspect, including chemical herbicides, insecticides, secondhand smoke, radiation exposure, and certain viruses.

The American Veterinary Medical Association lists the 10 Early Warning Signs of Cancer:

- Abnormal swellings that persist or continue to grow
- Sores that do not heal
- Weight loss
- Loss of appetite
- Bleeding or discharge from any body opening
- Offensive odor
- Difficulty eating or swallowing
- Hesitation to exercise or loss of stamina
- Persistent lameness or stiffness
- Difficulty breathing, urinating, or defecating
- As with humans, the survival rate for cancer victims has increased as new medicines and treatment protocols are having a positive effect. The key to winning this battle is early detection and professional treatment.

Kidney Failure

Increased water intake and urination could be a sign of the kidneys weakening. If the urine is clear and odorless, it may indicate that the kidneys are not removing the toxins from the system and that they are failing. Other symptoms might include diarrhea, vomiting, weight loss, fatigue, and lethargic behavior.

There are two basic types of kidney failure: chronic failure and sudden onset. Sudden onset is most often associated with some form of poisoning or dehydration. It can also be triggered by a heart attack, infection, heatstroke, or other causes. Whatever the cause, sudden onset kidney failure is most often treatable, depending on the severity of the cause, and should be attended to as an emergency.

Chronic kidney failure is an ongoing condition involving a birth defect (kidney dysplasia), immune system disease, cancer, or a parasitic problem. These causes can be treated if found early but may not be reversible.

Bloat/Torsion

Bloat is the retention of gas in the stomach, and torsion is the turning of the stomach into a position where the gas cannot escape. This illness will show itself with a tightened and bloated abdomen and attempts to vomit with nothing but frothy saliva come out. This is an extreme emergency requiring veterinarian intervention immediately. Usually surgery is performed within an hour of the initial symptoms or death will occur.

This disease affects deep-bodied larger-breed dogs more than smaller dogs and is found in German Shepherds with some frequency. Although there are a few large breeds with a far greater incidence of this problem, it is worth knowing about in this breed, for quick action is essential.

One of the most frequent problems with this disease is the lack of awareness on the part of some in the veterinary medical community. Most veterinary medical training is general and does not always give the doctor breed-specific information. As a good preventive measure, be sure your veterinarian is aware of this problem in the German Shepherd and has some experience with the surgical procedures to deal with it.

It would also be good to find out how your veterinary clinic handles emergencies. If there is an emergency clinic in your town, then contacting them to discuss their treatment protocol would be of value.

When bloating/torsion occurs, it is an extreme emergency and the victim will die within an hour or so if not treated. The treatment involves surgery, and the prevention of further life-threatening events can be effected by tacking the stomach so that it cannot turn over when the bloat occurs.

Stroke

A stroke may have many symptoms, including the pupils of the eyes being unequal in size and reacting differently to light. Your dog may also stumble, and you may find him standing in a corner or against a wall, pressing his head into the wall for stability. This also requires immediate veterinary care.

As in human medicine, great strides have occurred in the treatment of stroke. It need not be a death sentence if discovered and treated early. New medicines are available that can help reduce the clotting and return normal blood flow to the affected parts of the brain.

Heart Disease

Heart disease is a broad issue that is more common in import lines than in domestic lines, but is something one should watch for. A heart attack in a dog is much the same as in a human. Shortness of breath, panting, the inability to walk or to get up on things—all may show the presence of pain and discomfort. Immediate medical care is essential for this illness also. Heart medication for dogs follows the same general goal as human treatment. If you suspect something of this nature, you have the opportunity to alter his diet, exercise, and environmental setting, to make him more comfortable and increase his time with you.

And others...

There are many other diseases that can happen in the later years for our beloved dogs. Some are treatable and can allow him to function well, but none are to be ignored. This is certainly not a complete list of possibilities, but they are more common in the German Shepherd than others.

Common Health Issues

In addition to the emergency issues of a serious nature, there are things that are common to old age that may have no sure treatment protocol, but need to be acknowledged and investigated to see if they are simply the unavoidable consequences of age or have some underlying problem that needs to be addressed. They might include the following:

Hearing Loss

As with his human counterpart, the dog can lose part of his hearing ability as time marches on. Learning to speak louder or to go into the room where he is to talk to him can help keep him informed about your presence and what you are asking of him. This is one of the reasons for teaching hand signals in obedience training. You can reinforce your commands and desires to him with the hand signals. A gentle touch can also communicate your presence and your desired direction.

Vision Loss

The loss of clear vision at various distances is not uncommon for the canine species, so watch for signs of deteriorating vision. You can help him compensate by not rearranging the furniture without his knowledge and by making

FYI: Seeking Comfort

Most people liken the severity of losing a pet to losing a child or a mate. The degree of pain is the counterpart to the degree of love and enjoyment experienced in his life. So searching out professional care or grieving support is neither weak nor something about which to be embarrassed. There are a number of resources available, including talking to your breeder. They will understand. Here are some of those resources:

- The Association for Pet Loss and Bereavement—*www.aplb.org*
- The Loss Support Page—*www.pet-loss.nct*
- Rainbows Bridge—*www.rainbowsbridge.com*
- Pet Loss Grief Support—*www.petloss.com*

sure that he is not startled by some abrupt movement or person. Also check his eyes for any clouding that might occur.

Some canine vision problems can be successfully treated. Panus, the clouding of the eye, usually in high-elevation environments, is treatable with cyclosporine eye drops and can have a rather dramatic effect if used frequently. Canine cataracts can be treated in ways similar to human treatments.

Canine Dementia

Just as our minds can suffer from plaque and loss of memory, so can the aging dog's. He can become confused, disoriented, and frustrated. Although medication can help to restore a relatively normal life, it is not something to be ignored. Some dogs are gracious and easy in temperament, but some may turn their confusion and frustration into an angry array of actions. It is good to be aware and to be able to help him when he needs it.

There are many signs that he is experiencing dementia, but here are seven of the most common:

1. Confusion
2. Becoming less responsive
3. Forgetfulness
4. Wandering through the house
5. Getting lost in corners
6. Having accidents in the house
7. Not responding when his name is called

You may also notice abnormal sleeping patterns, unusual barking or licking, or other "nuisance" behavior. The good thing is that there are some newer medications that can help for some cases of dementia and restore normal brain function to some degree. If you suspect that he is losing his cognitive abilities, check with your veterinarian for confirmation and treatment.

Helping Your Senior Dog Cope

As your dog ages, you may find him more insecure and needing more attention and care. This can be a confusing time for him as he experiences the loss of physical abilities that have been his means of experiencing his life and reality. When he cannot run, jump, and play as he always has in the past, he may need a lot of reassurance that he is okay and still valued by you, the master. You are the focal point of his life, and your reaction to his condition is important to him. While he may be only a part of your life, you are his whole life.

With that in mind, plan to give extra time and care as his age takes from him his range of motion and his vigor. He will reward you a thousand times over with a nearness and devotion that only an old dog can provide. Be patient with him, keeping in mind that we all, human and dog, come to this point in life.

Tragically, many senior dogs are abandoned in their old age by those to whom these majestic dogs have given their lives and loyalties. The phenomenon is beyond the understanding of many, but it exists nonetheless. The cute little playful puppy grows quickly into an adult dog and a continuing responsibility that demands time and effort. Then the adult grows oh so quickly into a senior who needs more care and generates increased medical expenses. Soon, the youthful asset becomes a senior liability, and those who brought him home for the fun of it are no longer having fun with him. He is set aside to live out his remaining years in a shelter or rescue facility. This should never happen to any breed, let alone the majestic German Shepherd.

If and when the time comes that his quality of life is such that he no longer can enjoy it or cope with it, help him find the peace that further life cannot afford. Do not abandon him to find his way alone. He would never do that to you.

Saying Good-bye

I am not good at saying good-bye. Each time, I swear I will never have another dog. That commitment lasts at least three months, maybe six until I realize that the joy of living with a German Shepherd outweighs the pain of losing him. In fact, *"there is no pain where there has been no value, no loss where there has been no joy."*

The difficult thing is in knowing when to say good-bye. It is not an easy decision, for seldom is there clear cut criteria presented to our weary hearts as we wrestle with the question of when. The best we can do, and greatest measure we can allow ourselves to be judged by, is the question of what is best for him. When is life, as he has known it, so painful and terminal that he can no longer reasonably recover or enjoy it?

We do not have that option with our human family, and we leave them in the hands of modern medicine to ease their pain and hope for the best. But our culture, for whatever reason, has given to us the responsibility of determining the end of life for our pets. It is a responsibility that none of us enjoy and that no one ever wants to face. But just as certain as the joy he has given us is the knowledge that he will also tear our heart out with his leaving. Few experiences in life will bring the grief and sense of loss as losing a beloved best canine friend.

When it is time, and only you will know that time, the veterinarian will use a two-step process. The first shot will bring unconscious sleep, and the second will stop his heart, ending his life. The important thing to know is that his life, as he has known it and as he lived it, was over before that decision was made. Dogs live far less in their minds than we do. They live in the moment and in the experiences they have in their world of movement, in seeing the world around them, smelling the fragrances they encounter, hearing the sounds of nature and of their family. They live to experience their senses in the moment. To be deprived of that by illness or injury is not life. When recovery is no longer possible, it is humane to let them go.

Helpful Hints

Crying is a common human phenomenon and helps heal the emotions, the spirit, and the body. There is no embarrassment in crying when there is a great loss in life and no need to refrain when it is simply appropriate and needed. Besides, it is free, easily available, and has no side effects, except to one's makeup. So, if you feel inclined, go ahead!

My rule of thumb is that I will never make that decision for my convenience or welfare; it will always be for their welfare. One veterinarian shared with me the reasons some people have brought their pets to her for euthanasia. "We are leaving on vacation and he is old anyway." "He is not fun anymore and I need to go on with my life." And the list goes on with stupid and inane reasons for wanting to have a pet put down. If you do not have high regard for animals and particularly the German Shepherd, please buy a dog statue and leave the real dogs to those of us who care.

When the time comes, I have a ritual I will describe to you. How you handle it is of course a personal matter, but this is my pattern. I do not ask my friend to face this time of confusion and pain alone. I go with him into the veterinarian's office, or if he cannot walk, I park at the rear of the Veterinary hospital and the doctor comes out to give the shots. I talk with him about all the good times we've had together and all the shows we've been to. We share in that moment the good times of adventure and joy as I pet him and rub his head. Fortunately, our veterinarian is familiar with this pattern and stands away and gives me time to talk and love on him.

Then I nod to the doctor and she comes and administers the shots. I do not leave, but hold him in my arms as he slips away. I could not leave him at this time, for he would never leave me in difficult times or abandon me to a fate he would not face with me. We face his death together as we have faced life together.

He is always on his favorite blanket, and I wrap him carefully in it and take him for his final trip home. It really does not matter what happens to the physical body that remains, in my philosophy of life. It matters only that the memories remain and that he is respected for what he was. We are fortunate to have some acreage north of town and have marked off a plot for our cemetery. When we arrive home, he remains wrapped and in the car he so dearly loved to ride in while I get out the old tractor and dig an appropriate grave, and a hole at the head of the grave. The hole is for a tree that I have usually bought beforehand. He is lowered into the grave and covered with due respect, still in his favorite blanket. Then we plant the tree and extend the irrigation lines to it. Then I walk through the cemetery and talk to each of those who have left us and remember their lives and personalities and remember the glory of their presence and the pleasure they each brought to our house.

I cry a lot through this whole process and I am not ashamed of even one tear. It matters not what anyone thinks, for this is my life and this is my loss, and I make the most of it as I choose.

Then, as a final act of saying good-bye, I write him a letter or create for him a poem or document of my final thoughts. Much of this he will never know for he is gone, but I know, and I find some way to memorialize this wonderful life that has been shared so freely with me. I will not allow him to be forgotten.

Dealing with Grief

In time your emotions will be less fragile and your attention will refocus on other things, but the sense of loss will never go away. Don't expect it to right away. You will stumble over a toy, or find something that is a trigger and you will remember, and maybe even cry. It is good to allow yourself to experience the grief. It will lessen as time goes by, and in its place will come fond memories that will make you smile, even laugh. Grief is like a pond of water into which you occasionally throw a rock. The ripples from that rock will reverberate outward with intensity for a while, but with time they will lessen in intensity and in frequency until finally, after time has worked on it, the pond is placid again, leaving only the memories. That is a good time, a very

good time, when memories bring no pain but do bring a smile of remembered love and good adventures. The value of those times surely outweighs the pain of loss.

If you feel the need, you might want to call your breeder or veterinarian to talk about it. There are a lot of people in the dog world who will understand and will not mind listening to your stories and your memories. Creating a support group for a while is not a bad thing, and no one will feel taken advantage of by your doing so.

Moving On

No one will be able to tell you what to do next. Some people decide that the pain of loss is too great and that they will never have another dog. That is always my conclusion, but of course, it lasts only until I see that lovely little bundle of fur looking up at me with pleading eyes, saying, "Pick me. Pick me."

Only you can decide when and if you will have another dog and what breed it will be. For me, there is only one breed—the German Shepherd. Maybe it would be good to wait awhile, a year, a few months, or a few days… Only you will know. But when you find yourself reading through the want ads in the paper and wandering to the pets section, don't be afraid. Somewhere out there is another adventure that will bring you as much joy and love as your last one. Possibly it is a prizewinning puppy, waiting to lure you into the show ring, or an abandoned senior needing your love and care. Go ahead and look around, and as you do, be prepared for one little face to reach inside your chest and touch your heart. *Life can be no better than to begin all over again.*

Resources

Kennel and Breed Clubs

German Shepherd Dog Club
of America
10407 Springwood Drive
Spotsylvania, VA 22553
(540) 785-9292
All volunteer staff—no office hours
http://gsdca.org

American Kennel Club
8051 Arco Corporate Drive, Suite 100
Raleigh, NC 27617-3390
(919) 233-9767
Office hours: 8:30 AM–5:00 PM
(Monday–Friday)
www.akc.org

German Shepherd Dog Club
of America
Working Dog Association
732 Lindley Boulevard
DeLand, FL 32724
(386) 736-2486
www.gsdca-wda.org

American German Shepherd
Rescue Association
www.agsra.com

German Shepherd Dog Club of
America
Regional Clubs
*www.gsdca.org/join-the-gsdca/
regional-clubs*

United Kennel Club
100 E. Kilgore Road
Kalamazoo, MI 49002-5584
(269) 343-9020
www.ukcdogs.com

United Schutzhund Clubs
of America
3810 Paule Avenue
St. Louis, MO 63125-1718
*http://germanshepherddog.com/index.
html*

Note: There are numerous all-breed
registries and breed-specific registries available for the dog owner. It
is not our intention to leave any out
or to approve or disapprove of any.
An Internet search is the best way to
find these other sources.

German Shepherd Forums and Online Discussion Groups

Showgsd-l
www.showgsd.org

Gsdshowlist
www.gsdshowlist.org/index.html

gsdbydesign
www.gsdbydesign.com

Periodicals

GSD Review
www.gsdca.org/gsd-review

The German Shepherd Quarterly
www.hoflin.com

Health-Related

American Veterinary Medical
Association
www.avma.org

Orthopedic Foundation for Animals
www.offa.org/index.html

UC Davis School of Veterinary
Medicine
www.vetmed.ucdavis.edu

ASPCA Poison Control Center
www.aspcapro.org/animal-poison-control
(888) 426-4435

Canine Eye Registration Foundation
www.vmdb.org

University of Missouri College
of Veterinary Medicine
www.cvm.missouri.edu

American Kennel Club Health
Foundation
www.akcchf.org

Purina Dog Health
www.purina.com

Dog Health Guide
www.dog-health-guide.org

Dog Customer
http://www.dogcustomer.com

Training and Activities
American Kennel Club Canine
Good Citizen
www.akc.org/events/cgc

German Shepherd Club of America
Temperament Testing
www.gsdca.org/events/junior-handling

German Shepherd Club of
America-WDA
www.gsdca-wda.org/wda_new/EVENTS.html

United Schutzhund Clubs
of America
http://germanshepherddog.com/index.html

DVG America
www.dvgamerica.com

AKC Tracking
www.akc.org/events/tracking

AKC Rally
www.akc.org/events/rally

AKC Agility
www.akc.org/events/agility

National 4-H Program
http://4-h.org

Therapy Dogs International
www.tdi-dog.org

Delta Society
www.deltasociety.org

Association of Pet Dog Trainers
www.apdt.com

Pet Loss and Grief Support
Rainbows Bridge
www.rainbowsbridge.com

Association for Pet Loss
and Bereavement
www.aplb.org

Pet Loss Support Page
www.pet-loss.com

Pet Loss Grief Support
www.petloss.com

Travel Resources

Pets Welcome
www.petswelcome.com

Pet Airways
http://petairways.com

Pet Movers
www.petmovers.com

Pet Flight Information
www.petflight.com

Official Pet Hotels
www.officialpethotels.com

Dog Friendly
www.dogfriendly.com

Travel Pets
www.travelpets.com

National Association of Professional
Pet Sitters
www.petsitters.org

Pet Sitters International
www.petsit.com

Resource Books

Altman, Ginny and Hegewald-Kawich, Horst. *A Complete Pet Owner's Manual: German Shepherd Dogs.* Hauppauge, NY: Barron's Educational Series, Inc., 2006.

Moses, James A. and Strickland Gibson, Winfred. *The German Shepherd Dog Today.* New York, NY: Howell Book House, 1998.

Palika, Liz. *The German Shepherd Dog.* Neptune, NJ: Howell Book House, 1995.

Index

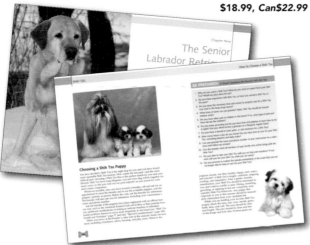

THE TEAM BEHIND THE *TRAIN YOUR DOG* DVD

Host **Nicole Wilde** is a certified Pet Dog Trainer and internationally recognized author and lecturer. Her books include *So You Want to Be a Dog Trainer* and *Help for Your Fearful Dog* (Phantom Publishing). In addition to working with dogs, Nicole has been working with wolves and wolf hybrids for over fifteen years and is considered an expert in the field.

Host **Laura Bourhenne** is a Professional Member of the Association of Pet Dog Trainers, and holds a degree in Exotic Animal Training. She has trained many species of animals including several species of primates, birds of prey, and many more. Laura is striving to enrich the lives of pets by training and educating the people they live with.

Director **Leo Zahn** is an award winning director/cinematographer/editor of television commercials, movies, and documentaries. He has directed and edited more than a dozen instructional DVDs through the Picture Company, a subsidiary of Picture Palace, Inc., based in Los Angeles.

Mokena Community
Public Library District